MISSION
Possible!

INSIGHT PUBLISHING
SEVIERVILLE, TENNESSEE

Published by Insight Publishing Company
P.O. Box 4189
Sevierville, Tennessee 37864

10 9 8 7 6 5 4 3 2

Printed in The United States of America

ISBN: 1-60013-

Table Of Contents

A Message From The Publisher...vii

Jeanne Hauer.. 1

Dr. Stephen R. Covey 15

Rhonda S. Jones..27

Tony Magee 45

Valarie Eiland Davis 63

Brian Tracy 79

Gail Kasper, LLC...91

Tom Bay, Ph.D. 105

Scott McFall 117

Jerry Stein 131

Ava Diamond 145

A Message From The Publisher

It's hard to believe that this is the tenth volume in our *Mission Possible!* series. When Volume I of the series was published in 2002, I predicted it would be a valuable resource. Each successive volume has proved that prediction to be accurate. Every chapter in this series has provided new insights on how to make what may seem like a mission impossible a mission possible.

Inside this anthology are conversations with successful people whose experiences provide fresh perspectives on reaching goals that initially appear beyond reach.

Between the covers of this book you will also find discussions about developing the basic principles of trustworthiness, honesty, caring, service, growth, and development. These principles are intrinsic to achieving success. As Dr. Stephen Covey says, "Good mentors teach principles rather than practices so that rules don't take the place of human judgment" (Chapter Two).

Why miss out on some of the most reliable information available about succeeding?

Go ahead, turn the page—keep turning and reading. You'll be glad you did!

Interviews conducted by:
David E. Wright
President, International Speakers Network

Chapter 1

JEANNE HAUER

THE INTERVIEW

David Wright (Wright)

Today we're talking with Jeanne Hauer. Jeanne is an author, speaker, and marketing/communications professional with a twenty-five-year track record working with individuals and businesses to maximize their success through "Peak Performance Marketing." Her signature approach uses the synergy of high performance and effective marketing communication to help organizations define their objectives, articulate their vision of success, and ultimately meet and exceed their goals.

Jeanne's book, *Millionaire Women—Success Secrets of 16 Who Made It from Home,* taps into her experience with entrepreneurs and corporations, and offers success secrets identified by sixteen high achieving women entrepreneurs whose stories are featured in her book. The result is a success blueprint for anyone hoping to advance a significant goal. Jeanne speaks to business, entrepreneur, and women's groups across the United States on goal-setting, success secrets, peak performance sales, and marketing solutions.

Jeanne, welcome to *Mission Possible!*

Jeanne Hauer (Hauer)

It's great to be here, David, to share ideas with you.

Wright

I am intrigued by your work identifying success secrets in your first book. How did you uncover these keys to achievement?

Hauer

My career as a marketing and business development professional has been focused on working with high-achieving individuals and businesses. Over the years I have observed best practices that seemed to be common among top performers. When I began interviews of successful women entrepreneurs for my *Millionaire Women* book, many of these winning approaches were in play yet again. As disciplines began to appear over and over in peak performance scenarios, it was obvious to me that they were at the heart of success secrets that would be of value to others.

Wright

Would you share a success secret before we hear more about your *Mission Possible* research?

Hauer

Of course. Although it is difficult to fully capture the essence out of the context of reading the *Millionaire Women* book, one of the success secrets I found thought-provoking and fundamental is: attitude is everything. This is so basic, but it is a discipline often very difficult to keep in focus. What we think about and how we feel about our lives sets the stage for everything. Positive attitude is a lifetime requirement for maximum success.

Wright

Was this secret common to all of the millionaire women in your book?

Hauer

All of the millionaire women were acutely aware of their own attitudes, goals, and dreams as they consciously worked to create the unique story of their own success. Although this "secret" may appear obvious, it takes commitment and discipline to maintain a positive attitude when challenges arise, as they always will. The founder of

Discovery Toys, Lane Nemeth, is a living example of a positive attitude. She considered the challenges she encountered in founding and growing her business to be "learning moments" rather than obstacles to her success. That is the power of positive attitude personified.

Wright

I understand that you tap into success secrets such as this and others every day in your own career. Furthermore, with twenty-five years as a marketing communications professional and with a lifetime study of the dynamics of success, you've developed the concept of "Peak Performance Marketing." What does this concept mean and who needs Peak Performance Marketing?

Hauer

Throughout my career, I have studied success, the habits of high achievers, and the dynamics of peak performance. I have analyzed what great success is and what it takes to achieve it. As my career unfolded in marketing, it occurred to me that the same principles of high achievement guiding successful people's everyday life would make an equally profound impact in someone's business life.

The combination of principles of peak performance and excellence applied to marketing is a powerful formula. I have counseled organizations and individuals over the years on how important it is that a product or service be excellent and that a marketing communications plan be launched for strategic visibility of that excellence. It is never enough to have just one or the other—great products or great visibility. The fact is that you have to have both for maximum business success. It is that combination of peak performance in products or services and a great marketing plan that makes the difference. Everyone in business can benefit from this approach.

Wright

Tell me more about your book, *Millionaire Women—Success Secrets of 16 Who Made it from Home*, and the messages you share in your speaking engagements about this book and its impact.

Hauer

Writing this book was a logical extension of my research on peak performance in business. I wrote *Millionaire Women* to encourage women of all ages, or any individual, to follow their dreams. As I looked at women in business and reflected on my own career I wondered who the high-achieving women were and how they combined the demands of their personal and professional lives to reach the highest levels of success. Could they have it all? In researching women who started a business from home that reached a million dollars in annual sales, it became apparent to me that these would be the women to study so that we might learn from their success.

With that in mind, I identified sixteen women who grew home-based businesses into major successes. The group included twelve women from across the United States and four from international companies located in Australia, South Africa, Canada, and the Netherlands. Some of these companies are well-known including Pampered Chef, Two Men and a Truck, Hanna Andersson, Discovery Toys, Vera Bradley, Schoolbelles, Cookies By Design, and Lillian Vernon. Others were smaller regional companies of high achievement.

I conducted interviews with the founders in order to share their stories. I asked each of them to describe what they did that made them successful and what motivations and principles drove their performance. Then, I analyzed the success secrets they had in common. Those are the messages I have shared in my speaking engagements. People are very interested to hear these inspiring and endearing stories of success and to learn from them.

Wright

Obviously, my company created the *Mission Possible!* book to bring together a collection of great ideas on the topic of success. But tell me, what motivated you to be part of *Mission Possible*?

Hauer

Mission Possible! is a wonderful step moving forward from my first book. While *Millionaire Women* looked at women in business and drew out common success secrets from the experience of women entrepreneurs, the *Mission Possible!* book gives us an expanded opportunity to speak to everyone—to every man and every woman— and to show how to take this wisdom beyond just business to a personal level. What is an individual's mission in life? What is the scope of his or her reach? When you consider these two concepts simultaneously, David, it is a powerful combination as people seek to realize their own potential. And of course, it has great popular appeal because of the whole *Mission Impossible!* pop media, movies, and culture around that. So, it speaks to people.

Wright

What does "Mission Possible" mean to you?

Hauer

As I think about Mission Possible, I am immediately reminded of the power of vision. Did you know that when the cities of ancient Rome and Athens were first founded, they were driven by the imagination and the vision of the leaders of those days? These leaders imagined great centers of enterprise including the arts—great cultural centers. It is an inspiration even today to see that these great cities could be created with the sheer force of vision even without all the technology we rely on now.

Let's recall the founding of our nation. The United States was created from the vision of pioneers looking for a land of freedom from oppression. Setting off in a wooden ship to sail across an ocean to an unknown land speaks volumes about the power of vision. People were willing to risk their lives for something more—and it became a mission possible.

Today, as we talk about space travel, cloning, and nanotechnology we can encourage one another to dream big and allow our minds to go forward with great ideas for improving the quality of life. This is really a very inspiring time to be alive. As a speaker and as an author, the whole Mission Possible concept really struck a chord.

Wright

How did your career as a professional speaker get started?

Hauer

Teachers and families often encourage young people to develop their unique skills and talents. As a young child, my friends and I used to put on little recitals in the back yard for our parents and relatives. Neighborhoods back then didn't have a lot of organized sports or other activities, so if someone had a dance lesson and they had costumes, we all performed and sang. It was just part of growing up in the Baby Boomer era. Later, as a young adult, I was encouraged by my parents and teachers to get involved in speech and drama in my high school.

As I grew older and my communication skills became a personal strength, I continued to develop my performance in public speaking. In my career as a marketing professional, I developed specializations in real estate, healthcare, and telecommunications business development.

To maximize the impact of my strategic marketing initiatives I was often asked to train sales organizations. As a skilled communicator, I knew this was a natural fit. Likewise, I was frequently asked to share my marketing knowledge within the company, and to present to external audiences when the company needed a corporate spokesperson. Within my own early career, these skills continued to grow and get stronger. Over time as I became known as a worthwhile speaker, people asked me to address other groups. The first *Millionaire Women* book really gave momentum to all of that. Now I am perhaps best known as a motivational storyteller and inspirational speaker who offers hope and tools for personal and business success.

Wright

Tell me about the concept of "mission" as you see it.

Hauer

We all have gifts. I was blessed with communication skills. Other people have great technical skills. Some people are musically inclined. We all have different gifts. We are each unique and have individual roles in this world. I believe that we are all born with a distinct contribution to make. So mission, as I see it, is the work of discovering our role and in fulfilling it, adding value to the world. When each of us develops our own unique gifts or skills, we can add value to our life and make a difference in the world, which will make the world a better place.

Wright

What about people who are out of touch with their own purpose? Can you give them any counsel about how to find their life mission?

Hauer

Some people are afraid to introspect. They don't really want to look within because it might challenge them to change. People can be very change averse. Great philosophers have said that, "the unexamined life is not worth living." However, for some people, it is too terrifying to introspect because they are not ready—they cannot handle the consequences that might result.

A national study was conducted recently to ask people what would be the top drivers of happiness that would help to create a better life?

The two things that were at the top of the list, as one could imagine, were more money and more time. The third most popular answer was more "purpose" in life.

I found it to be very interesting that, in a very general research setting, people were asking for more purpose in life. While it may not be an immediate concern for everyone, there is a real groundswell of interest in understanding our purpose. Why were we put here, and more personally, why was I born are questions openly asked in reference to both business and private life. What is the work that I came into this world to do and how can I give something back? As businesses conduct vision and mission-based planning, these considerations have become mainstream in corporate America. However, I'm not sure that it's possible to put people in touch with their own purpose unless they're ready. On the other hand, I believe that personal introspection and continued study of individuals who do seem to have a sense of purpose is of great value.

Wright

As you see it, what are the limits of possibility? In other words, how far should a person reach? How far can we go with all of this?

Hauer

Those are great questions. One could claim that possibilities are endless and we are only limited by our own ability to conceive what the next vision, the next opportunity, the next nuance could be. But we do have to be sensitive to the fact that life is all about balance. I would say possibilities are limitless, but the path there requires balance.

You can think of life as a ladder. Imagine, as you're climbing and reaching for the next step, that you reach out too far and tip the whole thing over. This might lead you to stop reaching. So having some sense of anchoring—some steadiness—in the process of pushing limits is very, very important.

On the other hand, anyone who's achieved something really great has definitely put some time forth where they may have been somewhat out of balance. They may have had to come back to balance later like a runner who will sprint for a while and then will go back to a measured pace. It appears that eventually everyone finds his or her life rhythm. While the limits of possibility are endless, the need for balance and rhythm in the midst of it is what holds it all together.

Wright

Have you had any personal Mission Possible experiences? Would you tell our readers about some of those experiences and what you learned from them that might be valuable to others?

Hauer

My Mission Possible experiences have been terrific.

In 1990 I began the practice of writing my goals down. Prior to that time, I thought I was in touch with my own goals but they remained unwritten. Since I began writing my goals each year, my achievements and dreams in every aspect of my life have been unfolding with more momentum than I had ever expected. Whether it was career advancement, family wishes, or personal dreams, success followed me in all the areas in which I had written goals.

Current business literature cites a study of 1950 Yale graduates whose written goals were the single differentiating factor for the top percent of the class who had achieved significantly more than all the other students. Written goals are a Mission Possible discipline.

A specific personal Mission Possible experience for me is my accomplishment in authoring the *Millionaire Women* book. I wrote that book while working full-time and completing studies for my MBA degree. I graduated from the MBA program about six months before the book was completed. On the surface, all of that appears to be almost impossible to achieve. However, because it was aligned with my purpose and because it was a sprint at the time, anchored by balance I had the Mission Possible experience of achieving those goals.

This year, I will also be launching my online newsletter *Success on the Run* from my Web site, *www.jeannehauer.com*. I have learned that if you pace yourself and you write down your goals and dreams, your vision and mission can become a reality.

In my experience as a professional speaker, I am frequently asked to keep in touch with audience members; many have heard me speak on several occasions. They have expressed a desire to hear more about the topics of success, goal-setting, and the power of vision. This online newsletter will be the vehicle to keep positive attitudes and momentum flowing with new audiences and with those who have already asked to be included in the distribution.

Wright

What do you recommend to nonbelievers regarding the power of possibility, of an individual or group reaching for a seemingly unattainable goal?

Hauer

For nonbelievers it's like any other concept. People require a moment of readiness to be open to a new idea. I'm not sure you can convince a person who isn't open to something new.

As you look at the power of possibility, for the non-believer I would say that it's all about risk and reward. Perhaps they haven't identified their passion and their own motivation in life. If the skeptics were to identify what was really important to them, I would say they might be more open to the power of possibilities and would be motivated to look around and pursue their dream.

Some say that there are actually only two basic motivations: desire and fear. So often, when people don't want to consider the possibility of how great life could be, it may be because they're afraid that they'll fail or fail again. They may fear that in gaining one thing they may have to let go of the comfort of the familiar that is their day-to-day life now.

When a person's focus is on the one thing of importance that they desire, they may be more willing to go each step further to make their life a little better. Desire may push them into possibility thinking, as it were, when they are aware of or acting on what motivates them. The classic example of this is the story of a burning building. No one in his or her right mind would enter a burning building. However, if a parent realizes one of his or her children is trapped inside, it is often almost impossible to restrain a father or mother from rushing headlong back into the inferno to save the child. The motivation to save the child drives the parent to actions that he or she would never attempt without extreme motivation. So the power of motivation, whether fear or desire, cannot be minimized for believers and nonbelievers alike.

Wright

What advice would you give to someone with his or her own Mission Possible dream?

Hauer

Earl Nightingale really sums it up when he talks about what he sees as the world's greatest secret, "You move in the direction of your predominant thought." For any individuals with a Mission Possible dream, I encourage them to surround themselves with positive ideas to advance their own Mission Possible and to follow their dream. Just get started. As Nike would say, *Just Do It!* They'll be surprised, perhaps, when they just start acting on it, thinking about it, writing down their ideas and their plans, and seeking support from the positive people around them. It works like magic when we work on our dreams. Eventually—maybe not immediately—but eventually, they can make their dreams and their mission a reality.

Wright

What about Mission Possible for children? What, in your estimation, can we look forward to in the future?

Hauer

Mission Possible is a perfect inspiration for children. However, grownups who can nurture these bright futures will need to remember that *thoughts are things*. In fact, we empower our children or we hold them back by how we regard them and what we teach them.

If we share cause and effect, children learn a life of consequences—that good energy begets good energy and bad energy begets bad. Further, if we live life that way and share those values with them, children will have a foundation for understanding how life works.

From the empowerment standpoint, if we respect young people's ideas and nurture and encourage them, anything is possible. We need to expose children to learning new horizons while teaching them ways to keep themselves in balance. Children can be encouraged to write down their goals. Their Mission Possible dreams are important, because children are, of course, the future.

As parents we need to "catch" kids doing something right and celebrate their success so they can recognize their contributions and gifts. In addition to a good grade in school, a well-played game, a successful lemonade stand, or a well-run paper route, we can celebrate their insights into their goals, their values, and their growing understanding of their uniqueness within a peer group that rewards conformity.

While the dreams of youth are immature early on, these children will achieve their success in the future based on how we nurture them to be balanced people now. It is our responsibility as adults and role models to respect and encourage our young people. Mission Possible for children empowers them to see how they can make the world a better place.

Wright
What a great conversation. I've learned a lot here. As a matter of fact, I just realized how much you've encouraged me.

Hauer
Thank you. I believe that when we share motivations we are all enriched and that's what it's all about. That is why thousands of people have read my book and have attended my presentations. If someone is actively searching for their Mission Possible they may be open to guidance or a significant idea that strikes a chord and is life-altering on any given day for a reader or member of the audience. For me, part of my life mission is to facilitate a dialogue around purpose and human potential and to offer encouragement to others to follow their dreams.

Wright
I really appreciate your taking this much time with me to answer these questions today, and I know our readers will benefit immensely from them.

Hauer
It is a delight to be a part of this project, and I am thrilled that *Mission Possible!* is going to be available for everyone. It's all about helping each other since none of us could do it alone. Sharing the journey sweetens the successes we achieve.

Wright
Today we've been talking to Jeanne Hauer. Her strategic approach using the synergy of high performance and effective marketing in communications has helped organizations define their vision and ultimately meet and exceed their goals. Jeanne is a much sought-after speaker and can be reached through her Web site, www.jeannehauer.com.

Her book, *Millionaire Women,* as we have learned today, shares stories of ordinary people who achieved extraordinary success. The book also taps into Jeanne's career experience counseling entrepreneurs and corporations in business development. More of the success secrets like those she has shared with us here, identified by sixteen high achieving women entrepreneurs, are featured in her book—a blueprint for anyone hoping to advance their goals.

Jeanne, thank you so much for being with us today on *Mission Possible!*

Hauer

David, it was my pleasure. Thank you.

About The Author

Jeanne Hauer is an author, speaker and marketing/business development professional with over twenty years of experience helping companies and individuals reach maximum achievement. Her years of expertise in business development along with the research she conducted for her book, Millionaire Women—Success Secrets of 16 Who Made It from Home, are a rich backdrop for Jeanne's presentations to groups on topics related to business and personal success.

The hallmark of Jeanne's professional success combines the discipline of peak performance along with strategic sales and marketing approaches for a powerful combination she calls "Peak Performance Marketing." The combination of effective marketing, training, product development, and sales strategy is the foundation for Jeanne's highly successful approach which has driven continuous double-digit annual sales growth in health insurance, real estate, and telecommunications, while growing bottom line profits each year.

Audiences find Jeanne's presentations to be entertaining, thought-provoking, and valuable as she modifies her message most effectively to meet the specific needs of the group she is addressing. She is a member of the National Speakers Association and has spoken to business, civic and women's groups across the country on business and motivational topics including business development, goal-setting, networking, entrepreneurism, and success secrets.

Jeanne has won numerous awards for her business achievement and is the author of a monthly newsletter, Success on the Run, which is available from her Web site: www.jeannehauer.com.

Jeanne Hauer
Marketing Success Expert,
Author of Millionaire Women
Phone: 216-292-7833
E-mail: jeanne@jeannehauer.com
www.jeannehauer.com

Chapter 2

DR. STEPHEN R. COVEY

David Wright (Wright)
We're talking today with Dr. Stephen R. Covey, cofounder and vice-chairman of Franklin Covey Company, the largest management company and leadership development organization in the world. Dr. Covey is perhaps best known as the author of *The 7 Habits of Highly Effective People* which is ranked as a number one best seller by the *New York Times*, having sold more than fourteen million copies in thirty-eight languages throughout the world. Dr. Covey is an internationally respected leadership authority, family expert, teacher, and organizational consultant. He has made teaching principle-centered living and principle-centered leadership his life's work. Dr. Covey is the recipient of the Thomas More College Medallion for Continuing Service to Humanity and has been awarded four honorary doctorate degrees. Other awards given Dr. Covey include the Sikh's 1989 International Man of Peace award, the 1994 International Entrepreneur of the Year award, *Inc.* magazine's Services Entrepreneur of the Year award, and in 1996 the National Entrepreneur of the Year Lifetime Achievement award for Entrepreneurial leadership. He has also been recognized as one of *Time* magazine's twenty-five most influential Americans and one of Sales and Marketing Management's top

twenty-five power brokers. Dr. Covey earned his undergraduate degree from the University of Utah, his MBA from Harvard, and completed his doctorate at Brigham Young University. While at Brigham Young he served as assistant to the President and was also a professor of business management and organizational behavior. Dr. Covey, welcome to *Mission Possible!*

Dr. Stephen Covey (Covey)

Thank you.

Wright

Dr. Covey, most companies make decisions and filter them down through their organization. You, however, state that no company can succeed until individuals within it succeed. Are the goals of the company the result of the combined goals of the individuals?

Covey

Absolutely, because if people aren't on the same page they're going to be pulling in different directions. To teach this concept, I frequently ask large audiences to close their eyes and point north, and then to keep pointing and open their eyes and they find themselves pointing all over the place. I say to them, "Tomorrow morning if you want a similar experience, ask the first ten people you meet in your organization what the purpose of your organization is and you'll find it's a very similar experience. They'll point all over the place." When people have a different sense of purpose and values, every decision that is made from then on is governed by those. There's no question that this is one of the fundamental causes of misalignment, low trust, interpersonal conflict, interdepartmental rivalry, people operating on personal agendas, and so forth.

Wright

Is that mostly a result of the inability to communicate from the top?

Covey

That's one aspect, but I think it's more fundamental. There's an inability to involve people—an unwillingness. Leaders may communicate what their mission and their strategy is, but that doesn't mean there's any emotional connection to it. Mission statements that are rushed and then announced are soon forgotten. They become nothing more than just a bunch of platitudes on the wall that mean essentially nothing and even create a source of cynicism and a sense of hypocrisy inside the culture of an organization.

Wright

How do companies ensure survival and prosperity in these tumultuous times of technological advances, mergers, downsizing, and change?

Covey

I think that it takes a lot of high trust in a culture that has something that doesn't change—principles—at its core. There are principles that people agree upon that are valued. It gives a sense of stability. Then you have the power to adapt and be flexible when you experience these kinds of disruptive new economic models or technologies that come in and sideswipe you. You don't know how to handle them unless you have something you can depend upon. If people have not agreed to a common set of principles that guide them and a common purpose, then they get their security from the outside and they tend to freeze the structure, systems, and processes inside and they cease becoming adaptable. They don't change with the changing realities of the new marketplace out there and gradually they become obsolete.

Wright

I was interested in one portion of your book *The 7 Habits of Highly Effective People* where you talk about behaviors. How does an individual go about the process of replacing ineffective behaviors with effective ones?

Covey

I think that for most people it usually requires a crisis that humbles them to become aware of their ineffective behaviors. If there's not a crisis the tendency is to perpetuate those behaviors and not change. You don't have to wait until the marketplace creates the crisis for you. Have everyone accountable on a 360 degree basis to everyone else they interact with—with feedback either formal or informal—where they are getting data as to what's happening. They will then start to realize that the consequences of their ineffective behavior require them to be humble enough to look at that behavior and to adopt new, more effective ways of doing things. Sometimes people can be stirred up to this if you just appeal to their conscience—to their inward sense of what is right and wrong. A lot of people sometimes know inwardly they're doing wrong, but the culture doesn't necessarily discourage them from continuing that. They either need feedback from people, or they need feedback from the marketplace, or they need feedback from their conscience. Then they can begin to develop a step-by-step process of replacing old habits with new, better habits.

Wright

It's almost like saying, "Let's make all the mistakes in the laboratory before we put this thing in the air."

Covey

Right; and I also think what is necessary is a paradigm shift, which is analogous to having a correct map, say of a city or of a country. If people have an inaccurate paradigm of life, of other people, and of themselves it really doesn't make much difference what their behavior or habits or attitudes are. What they need is a correct paradigm—a correct map—that describes what's going on. For instance, in the Middle Ages they used to heal people through bloodletting. It wasn't until Samuel Weiss and Pasteur and other empirical scientists discovered the germ theory that they realized for the first time they weren't dealing with the real issue. They realized why women preferred to use midwives who washed rather than doctors who didn't wash. They gradually got a new paradigm. Once you've got a new paradigm then your behavior and your attitude flows directly from it. If you have a bad paradigm or a bad map, let's say of a city, there's no way, no matter what your behavior or your habits or your attitudes are—how positive they are—you'll never be able to find the location you're looking for. This is why I believe that to change paradigms is far more fundamental than to work on attitude and behavior.

Wright

One of your seven habits of highly effective people is to begin with the end in mind. If circumstances change and hardships or miscalculation occurs, how does one view the end with clarity?

Covey

Many people think to begin with the end in mind means that you have some fixed definition of a goal that's accomplished and if changes come about you're not going to adapt to them. Instead, the "end in mind" you begin with is that you are going to create a flexible culture of high trust so that no matter what comes along you are going to do whatever it takes to accommodate that new change or that new reality and maintain a culture of high performance and high trust. You're talking more in terms of values and overall purposes that don't change, rather than specific strategies or programs that will have to change to accommodate the changing realities in the marketplace.

Wright

In this time of mistrust between people, corporations, and nations for that matter, how do we create high levels of trust?

Covey

That's a great question and it's complicated because there are so many elements that go into the creating of a culture of trust. Obviously the most fundamental one is just to have trustworthy people. But that is not sufficient because what if the organization itself is misaligned? For instance, what if you say you value cooperation but you really reward people for internal competition? Then you have a systemic or a structure problem that creates low trust inside the culture even though the people themselves are trustworthy. This is one of the insights of Edward Demming and the work he did. That's why he said that most problems are not personal; they're systemic. They're common caused. That's why you have to work on structure, systems, and processes to make sure that they institutionalize principle-centered values. Otherwise you could have good people with bad systems and you'll get bad results.

When it comes to developing interpersonal trust between people, it is made up of many, many elements such as taking the time to listen to other people, to understand them, and to see what is important to them. What we think is important to another may only be important to us, not to another. It takes empathy. You have to make and keep promises to them. You have to treat them with kindness and courtesy. You have to be completely honest and open. You have to live up to your commitments. You can't betray them behind their back. You can't badmouth them behind their back and sweet-talk them to their face. That will send out vibes of hypocrisy and it will be detected. You have to learn to apologize when you make mistakes, to admit mistakes, and to also get feedback going in every direction as much as possible. It doesn't necessarily require formal forums; it requires trust between people that will be open with each other and give each other feedback.

Wright

My mother told me to do a lot of what you're saying now, but it seems like when I got in business I simply forgot.

Covey

Sometimes we forget, but sometimes culture doesn't nurture it. That's why I say unless you work with the institutionalizing—that means formalizing into structure, systems, and processes the values—you will not have a nurturing culture. You have to constantly work on that. This is one of the big mistakes organizations make. They think trust is simply a function of being honest. That's only one small aspect. It's an important aspect, obviously, but there are so many other elements that go into the creation of a high trust culture.

Wright

"Seek first to understand then to be understood" is another of your seven habits. Do you find that people try to communicate without really understanding what other people want?

Covey

Absolutely. The tendency is to project out of our own autobiography—our own life, our own value system—onto other people, thinking we know what they want. So we don't really listen to them. We pretend to listen, but we really don't listen from within their frame of reference. We listen from within our own frame of reference and we're really preparing our reply rather than seeking to understand. This is a very common thing. In fact very few people have had any training in seriously listening. They're trained in how to read, write, and speak, but not to listen.

Reading, writing, speaking, and listening are the four modes of communication and they represent about two-thirds to three-fourths of our waking hours. About half of that time is spent listening, but it's the one skill people have not been trained in. People have had all this training in the other forms of communication. In a large audience of 1,000 people you wouldn't have more than twenty people who have had more than two weeks of training in listening. Listening is more than a skill or a technique so that you're listening within another frame of reference. It takes tremendous courage to listen because you're at risk when you listen. You don't know what's going to happen; you're vulnerable.

Wright

Sales gurus always tell me that the number one skill in selling is listening.

Covey

Yes—listening from within the customer's frame of reference. That is so true. You can see that it takes some security to do that because you don't know what's going to happen.

Wright

With our *Mission Possible!* talk show and book we're trying to encourage people in our audience to be better, to live better, and be more fulfilled by listening to the examples of our guests. Is there anything or anyone in your life that has made a difference for you and helped you to become a better person?

Covey

I think the most influential people in my life have been my parents. I think that what they modeled was not to make comparisons and harbor jealousy or to seek recognition. They were humble people. I remember my mother one time when we were going up in an elevator and the most prominent person in the state was in the elevator. She knew him, but she spent her time talking to the elevator operator. I was just a little kid and I was so awed by this person and I said to my mom, "Why didn't you talk to the important person?" She said, "I was. I had never met him." They were really humble, modest people who were focused on service and other people rather than on themselves. I think they were very inspiring models to me.

Wright

In almost every research paper that anyone I've ever read writes about people who influenced their lives, in the top five people, three of them are teachers. My seventh grade English teacher was the greatest teacher I ever had and influenced me to no end.

Covey

Would it be correct to say that she saw in you probably some qualities of greatness you didn't even see in yourself?

Wright

Absolutely.

Covey

That's been my general experience that the key aspect of a mentor or a teacher is someone who sees in you potential that you don't even see in yourself. They treat you accordingly and eventually you come to see it in yourself. That's my definition of leadership or influence—communicating people's worth and potential so clearly that they are inspired to see it in themselves.

Wright

Most of my teachers treated me as a student, but she treated me with much more respect than that. As a matter of fact, she called me Mr. Wright in the seventh grade. I'd never been addressed by anything but a nickname. I stood a little taller; she just made a tremendous difference. Do you think there are other characteristics that mentors seem to have in common?

Covey

I think they are first of all good examples in their own personal lives. Their personal lives and their family lives are not all messed up—they come from a base of good character. They also are usually very confident and they take the time to do what your teacher did to you—to treat you with uncommon respect and courtesy.

They also, I think, explicitly teach principles rather than practices so that rules don't take the place of human judgment. You gradually come to have faith in your own judgment in making decisions because of the affirmation of such a mentor. Good mentors care about you—you can feel the sincerity of their caring. It's like the expression, "I don't care how much you know until I know how much you care."

Wright

Most people are fascinated with the new television shows about being a survivor. What has been the greatest comeback that you've made from adversity in your career or your life?

Covey

When I was in grade school I experienced a disease in my legs. It caused me to use crutches for a while. I tried to get off them fast and get back. The disease wasn't corrected yet so I went back on crutches for another year. The disease went to the other leg and I went on for another year. It essentially took me out of my favorite thing—athletics—and it took me more into being a student. So that was kind of a life-defining experience which at the time seemed very negative, but has proven to be the basis on which I've focused my life—being more of a learner.

Wright

Principle-centered learning is basically what you do that's different from anybody I've read or listened to.

Covey

The concept is embodied in the far-eastern expression, "Give a man a fish, you feed him for the day; teach him how to fish, you feed him for a lifetime." When you teach principles that are universal and timeless, they don't belong to just any one person's religion or to a particular culture or geography. They seem to be timeless and universal like the ones we've been talking about here: trustworthiness, honesty, caring, service, growth, and development. These are universal principles. If you focus on these things then little by little people become independent of you and then they start to believe in themselves and their own judgment becomes better. You don't need as many rules. You don't need as much bureaucracy and as many controls and you can empower people.

The problem in most business operations today—and not just business but non-business—is that they're using the industrial model in an information age. Arnold Toynbee, the great historian, said, "You can pretty well summarize all of history in four words: nothing fails like success." The industrial model was based on the asset of the machine. The information model is based on the asset of the person—the knowledge worker. It's an altogether different model. But the machine model was the main asset of the twentieth century. It enabled productivity to increase fifty times. The new asset is intellectual and social capital—the qualities of people and the quality of the relationship they have with each other. Like Toynbee said, "Nothing fails like success." The industrial model does not work in an information age. It requires a focus on the new wealth, not capital and material things.

A good illustration that demonstrates how much we were into the industrial model, and still are, is to notice where people are on the balance sheet. They're not found there. Machines are found there. Machines become investments. People are on the profit and loss statement and people are expenses. Think of that—if that isn't blood-letting.

Wright

It sure is.

When you consider the choices you've made down through the years, has faith played an important role in your life?

Covey

It has played an extremely important role. I believe deeply that we should put principles at the center of our lives, but I believe that God is the source of those principles. I did not invent them. I get credit sometimes for some of the Seven Habits material and some of the other things I've done, but it's really all based on principles that have been given by God to all of His children from the beginning of time. You'll find that you can teach these same principles from the sacred texts and the wisdom literature of almost any tradition. I think the ultimate source of that is God and that is one thing you can absolutely depend upon—in God we trust.

Wright

If you could have a platform and tell our audience something you feel would help them or encourage them, what would you say?

Covey

I think I would say to put God at the center of your life and then prioritize your family. No one on their deathbed ever wished they spent more time at the office.

Wright

That's right. We have come down to the end of our program and I know you're a busy person, but I could talk with you all day Dr. Covey.

Covey

It's good to talk with you as well and to be a part of this program. It looks like an excellent one that you've got going on here.

Wright

Thank you.

We have been talking today with Dr. Stephen R. Covey, co-founder and vice-chairman of Franklin Covey Company. He's also the author of *The 7 Habits of Highly Effective People,* which has been ranked as a number one bestseller by the *New York Times,* selling more than fourteen million copies in thirty-eight languages.

Dr. Covey, thank you so much for being with us today on *Mission Possible!*

Covey

Thank you for the honor of participating.

About The Author

STEPHEN R. COVEY was recognized in 1996 as one of *Time* magazine's twenty-five most influential Americans and one of Sales and Marketing Management's top twenty-five power brokers. Dr. Covey is the author of several acclaimed books, including the international bestseller, *The 7 Habits of Highly Effective People*. It has sold more than fifteen million copies in thirty-eight languages throughout the world. Other bestsellers authored by Dr. Covey include *First Things First, Principle-Centered Leadership*, with sales exceeding one million, and *The 7 Habits of Highly Effective Families*.

Dr. Covey's newest book, *The 8th Habit: From Effectiveness to Greatness*, which was released in November 2004, has risen to the top of several bestseller lists, including *New York Times, Wall Street Journal, USA Today, Money, Business Week*, and Amazon.com and Barnes & Noble. The *8th Habit* . . . has sold more than 360,000 copies.

Dr. Covey earned his undergraduate degree from the University of Utah, his MBA from Harvard, and completed his doctorate at Brigham Young University. While at Brigham Young University, he served as assistant to the President and was also a professor of business management and organizational behavior. He received the National Fatherhood Award in 2003, which, as the father of nine and grandfather of forty-four, he says is the most meaningful award he has ever received.

Dr. Covey currently serves on the board of directors for the Points of Light Foundation. Based in Washington, D.C., the Foundation, through its partnership with the Volunteer Center National Network, engages and mobilizes millions of volunteers from all walks of life—businesses, nonprofits, faith-based organizations, low-income communities, families, youth, and older adults—to help solve serious social problems in thousands of communities.

Dr. Stephen R. Covey
www.stephencovey.com

Chapter 3

RHONDA S. JONES

David Wright (Wright)

Rhonda Jones brings over two decades of international Fortune 100 leadership on both the planning and the implementation side of large-scale business improvement. Her extensive management knowledge and experience in both for-profit and non-profit organizations enable her to facilitate the development of high-performing *business communities*. Rhonda further applies an adult education background and understanding of group dynamics to build strong teams capable of delivering extraordinary results. Her unique ability to engage people at all levels of an organization, her practical, down-to-earth approach, and her use of humor, wit, and true stories, make her a dynamic and entertaining trainer and speaker and highly effective organizational consultant. She also writes about common sense principles for effective working and living.

Rhonda, welcome to *Mission Possible!*

Rhonda Jones (Jones)

Thank you, David.

Wright

Rhonda, you write and speak about using common sense in the workplace. Can you tell our readers a little bit about that?

Jones

Sure, David. I do focus on common sense, but not just in the workplace. Whether it's work or social, with colleagues, family, or friends, any mission is possible, if we just apply a little common sense. That's the whole purpose of humans having the ability to develop common sense.

Wright

What do you mean by that?

Jones

Common sense is *practical wisdom* derived from everyday experiences. It's the lessons we learn from everything we see, hear, and do each and every moment of each and every day. During my career, I found that the people who didn't learn from their so-called mistakes continued to have the same problems over and over. Where I grew up, the older people used to say, "She has to learn everything the *hard way.*" I finally realized that learning the *hard way* through learning from everything we see, hear, and do is actually the way we grow our common sense.

Wright

Yes, I've heard you say that we can "grow our common sense," and I want to come back to that. But first, you mentioned the place where you grew up. I've noticed that seems to play heavily in your writing, speaking, and teaching.

Jones

It does; that's certainly true. Since my book, *Teaching Common Sense,* has been published I've begun to elaborate on it more and more through teaching and speaking. I've come to the realization that the foundation for my management theories and for the book really did originate in that small country community where I grew up.

Wright

Why do you say that? You have a master's degree in education and have had a twenty-four-year career working all over the world. How is it that you can give credit to your youth on a little farm in the country?

Jones

There's no doubt I have definitely learned a great deal throughout my academic and business career. I feel very fortunate to have had those opportunities and experiences. I hope to continue to learn until the day I close my eyes for good. In fact, in the last few years, as a result of my focus on developing and teaching these theories, I've made it my mission to place myself in as many different cultural, economic, and social situations as possible to continue to expand my understanding of human interaction. But there are several reasons I can now look back and see the tremendous positive impact of my experiences in the country.

First, let me explain by telling you about my home. We lived about twenty-five miles from the nearest town, which wasn't very big either, but it did have a few traffic lights. It didn't matter, though, because I didn't get to see it much—maybe once or twice a year. Our county was the largest county in landmass in the state, so people lived pretty spread out from one another. I think that's why the little communities became such strong centers of daily life. If you asked someone where they were from, they wouldn't give you the name of the town or the county, they would give you the name of their community. They would say Glenwood or Orebank or St. James, Sunnyside, Greystone, Camp Creek, Ottway, West Pines, Baileyton or Cross Anchor. When you heard that community name, it meant something to you. It told you a lot about that person.

Wright

There are some people out there now who claim to be experts in "building community." Would you consider yourself an expert in that?

Jones

Yes, I would. I know there are others who approach this from a very theoretical or psychological perspective. We are all teaching the same thing and, quite frankly, we all have the same theoretical foundation. The difference I bring is my deeply embedded experience of living in community longer than some others have even been talking about it. It's a part of who I am, and I have tons of experience applying it socially and in business, so I'm able to give people the benefit of that wealth of experience. Plus, I've been told my experiences make my training quite interesting and often very entertaining.

The one point on which I think all of us agree is that building community is critical to an organization's success. We tend to define businesses by the products they sell or the services they provide. But the reality of business is that it's about the people. If you took the people away, it would all cease to exist. Businesses are communities of humans. Whether companies and organizations are intentional about building community or not, they have one, and it may be effective or it may be terribly ineffective. I know that all my corporate success has stemmed from my ability to build effective communities.

The understanding I gained for what makes a community effective, by growing up in it—learning it almost by osmosis, then applying it around the world for over two decades—is why I say the foundation of my work originated there. When I go into companies or organizations now, I instinctively look for those same signs of community. I check to see if, from talking to people and observing, I can determine the culture of their work community and whether it's conducive to achieving the goals they claim to be pursuing. In other words, I'm looking for congruence between what they say versus what they do, and what they say they value versus how it actually feels to be among them.

I specialize in helping teams, organizations, and businesses become intentional about diagnosing the true culture of their community, defining the culture they need, then doing the right things to build that community enabling the members to be capable of getting their particular jobs done in a mutually beneficial way. There are objective means for making this assessment, but in addition to that, I'm able to feel it and sense it in intangible ways. It sounds a little touchy-feely, but my approach resonates with even the most no-nonsense business veteran. I utilize years of project leadership experience to guide them through very specific business development activities.

Wright

So, what are those simple, down-to-earth clues of an effective community you look for?

Jones

There are a few key things about community I've learned from my life. First, everything in the community needs to "make sense." If I heard my Dad say that once, I must have heard it hundreds of times. "Why are you doing that, Rhonda?" he would ask, "That doesn't make sense." He trained me to analyze in advance the potential outcome of all my words, thoughts, and actions—to understand the cause and effect relationships that link everything together—in order to increase my probability of success with whatever I was doing. My whole theory of a common sense approach to life and work stems from those lessons he taught. Sometimes it drove me crazy for him to quiz me on it, but I realize now there was an important reason.

We had very limited resources in that small country community. We couldn't afford to act haphazardly or recklessly and waste those precious resources. There was no money to go out and buy more. Plus, if you made a mistake with the crops, you could destroy that season's entire harvest. That would have been devastating because we really did live from one harvest to the next. Always making the most sensible choice, which often meant asking for advice from more experienced people in the community, and then working hard to carry out those decisions was an important lesson I learned on a small farm in that country community. If you think about it, it's no different in companies or organizations where resources are always limited and efficient employee effort is critical.

Wright

What else did you learn about community that you think is important for businesses and organizations to know?

Jones

Well, I just mentioned there needs to be a prevailing *commonsense* approach to decision-making. Plus, I alluded to the fact that there's also visible evidence of a lot of *hard work* and effort being expended to carry out those decisions. An effectively functioning community doesn't just happen by accident. Once the best possible decisions have been made, you have to work the plan. Losing interest or focus during implementation defeats the whole decision-making process. Those are the first two factors. An additional eight factors turned a loose connection of farms into a *community*. I'll talk about each one but, in short, they are *purpose, spirit, expertise, abundance mentality, helping, self-sustaining, legends,* and *language*. All of these were not only critical to our little country community, but are also extremely critical to the success of businesses and organizations. I often use stories from my community to illustrate this. Let's look at each factor, starting with *purpose*.

The geographic center of our community was shaped like a diamond—the school and store were next door to each other on one corner, the Methodist church on another, the old country store on the third corner, and the community center and baseball field on the fourth corner. That area was the heart of our community and it was also very symbolic of the purpose of the community.

The purpose around which our whole community rallied was family and faith. Farming to feed and clothe the family, pay for the school to educate the children, and support the church to minister to the community's spiritual needs was a primary focus in the community. Everything in the community was aligned to that purpose. The country store stocked the kind of hardware, seed, grain, and supplies needed on the farms. And the church services and community dinners, picnics, and ballgames at the community center extended that sense of family from the individual farms to the community-at-large. We were one extended family, united around that common *purpose*.

In the same manner, for a business community to thrive it must have all its members rallied around a common purpose. Everyone needs to be pulling, pushing, and guiding the "wagon" in the same direction so to speak.

As a result of that commonly accepted purpose in the community where I lived, there was a prevailing *spirit* in the community. It was something you could both see and feel. People were proud to be a part of the community and they worked hard to live up to the values for which it stood. Farms were kept so neat and maintained; they were truly picturesque.

People dressed up to go to church or to the community center for a dinner or to the ball field for a baseball game on Sunday afternoon. Even if they didn't have much, they cleaned up as best they could. Some of the farmers would have one pair of good bib overalls they saved for these occasions. The denim was as dark blue as the day they were made and the fabric was still so stiff and straight, I believe you could have stood those overalls in the floor and they wouldn't have fallen over. It is kind of comical to think about it now. But seeing those old guys get fixed up like that taught me something about the spirit and pride of belonging to a community and always giving it your best.

Unfortunately, I often do not find that same spirit of pride and esprit de corps when I walk through some organizations. And if a person's spirit is not fully engaged, he or she won't be able to give you his or her best effort. It's the leader's job to create an environment to foster that.

Speaking of giving it your best, that leads me to the fifth key factor in building community, which I previously described as *expertise*. In the community the prevailing culture was one in which people simply did whatever it was they did best. There was one lady I remember who was always the event planner. If there was a dinner or picnic or covered-dish supper to be planned, in minutes she could pass out assignments for how many pounds of meat, mashed potatoes, corn and green beans, or potato salad, slaw and baked beans were needed and who should cook how much of what . . . not to mention the bread, cakes, pies, and homemade iced tea. Everyone knew that the wise thing to do, on these occasions, was to delegate that task to her, because she did it best.

There was another lady who was the resident expert whenever we needed to put on some kind of pageant or play or musical cantata. She led the adult and youth choir and organized all the ladies, men, and children of the community into production companies, singers, and actors as required. That's how it worked. If you were good at farming, then you farmed. If you were good at carpentry or plumbing, then you were a carpenter or plumber. If you could wire, then you were an electrician. If you had a welder and knew how to use it, then you were a welder. I even remember one man everyone called on when they needed to haul cattle to or from the stock market because he was the person in the community who had the trailer!

You weren't made to feel inadequate because, for instance, you didn't know how to weld or to plumb. It was understood and even expected that each individual would be different. The community was characterized by an environment in which each unique individual had the opportunity to contribute whatever he or she did best. That helped create a sense of pride because it gave everyone an equal chance to feel that he or she was an important and valued member of the community—it was clear to them how they fit in.

This may be the biggest problem I see in organizations. Employees haven't been correctly placed where they can personally flourish. They don't understand how their work is linked to the overall goals of the company and they don't know what they can do to help reach those goals. On top of that, their managers are not actively seeking to know what their talents are and what they are capable of, so their value is all too often lost.

If communities are able to create an environment in which each member feels they can contribute what they also love to do, one of the great results this fosters is an *abundance mentality*, which is factor number six. I've mentioned earlier that our resources were scarce. That was just a reality of life in the country. Nevertheless, not once did I ever feel deprived. We were always working hard to improve our farm and our community, yet there was always the feeling of "enough." We had a table full of fresh vegetables and meat and eggs from right there on the farm. Every meal was a feast. We had new clothes that Momma sewed by hand—custom tailored just for us.

There was always something going on at school or at church or at the community center to bring us together and keep us entertained. And, if you just wanted to "loafer" there was always an empty seat on the bench at the country store where you could sit and visit for a spell while enjoying a "yeller dope and a moon pie." No one felt like they were missing out on anything. Most people never even wanted to leave the community, even when the opportunity presented itself. There was a prevailing feeling of abundance. Consequently, no one was jealous or covetous of another. Each had their own specialty, their own identity, their own prosperity, and everyone understood that it all worked together for the good of the community. So, instead of tearing one another down, effort was aimed at building one another up.

Too many times in organizations I see a scarcity mentality. People hoard knowledge and don't share what they know with co-workers because they somehow feel this hoarded knowledge is their security or they incorrectly think their success, recognition, or promotion can only come at the expense of those around them. Often their leaders simply haven't created a safe environment in which they can express themselves. However, by operating with that mentality they are actually destroying their security because they are undermining the effectiveness of the company and its chances for success. If the community doesn't turn that scarcity mentality into an abundance mentality, then this negative, scarcity type of thinking will become a self-fulfilling prophecy.

That leads to the seventh factor of *helping*. In the community, neighbors helped neighbors. Referring back to the comments I made about different skills, everyone in the community helped everyone else by sharing their expertise, resources, and prosperity. If a farmer had a banner year in corn or hay, for instance, but a neighbor had a bad crop, they would share the excess. Everyone in the community called on the person who was a carpenter or plumber or electrician whenever they needed that kind of help. Sometimes a little token money exchanged hands, but usually it was just taken out in trade. It all centered around the abundance mentality of the community. *I'll give you some hay to feed your cattle this winter, if you'll haul some of my cattle to market. I'll give you some corn for some green beans.*

Everyone took pride in their ability to help their neighbors. The most obvious examples were when a family was struck by an unfortunate injury, illness, or death. The whole community would rally around them and do whatever was needed—cook food, milk the cows, tend or harvest the crops, re-build the barn—sometimes for weeks, months or even years on end. It might be something as simple as taking groceries to shut-ins. In one way or another—both large and small—people in the community helped one another by sharing their expertise, resources, and abundance.

That's what companies must do. The whole must be greater than the sum of its parts. Team members must be able and willing to pick up the slack for another team member when the need arises. It's the visible sign of expertise and abundance mentality in action. This too must be enabled by leaders who create the right environment for it to become commonplace. When a community is characterized by a culture of helping, that leads to the eighth factor I look for.

The eighth factor of community is that it is able to be *self-sustaining*. As I mentioned earlier, people in the community didn't waste time thinking about what they didn't have. They didn't sit around feeling sorry for themselves for having it so tough, while their farms fell down dilapidated around them. On the contrary, there was a constant hum of what I call *happy industry*. My Daddy wasn't much of a singer, but I still remember hearing him singing over the sound of the tractor and the hay rake behind it as he went round and round under the broiling sun in the dusty hay field. Workers would come shuffling in from the fields covered in dirt and sweat for a cold drink at the store or a hot, home-cooked meal in the country kitchen. The women, when they weren't in the fields, would slave over hot stoves in kitchens that were not air-conditioned to can, pickle, and preserve the farm produce to feed their families.

There was an awful lot of work to be done in the spring to plant and then in the summer and fall to harvest and preserve, mainly to prepare for winter. In winter there was more work to be done cutting firewood and feeding livestock and poultry. Yet, through all that hard work there was laughter and happiness. There was always joy, if only in the simplest things, and that joyous industry sustained the community year after year, generation after generation.

The focus of the members of the community was always on how to carry on this legacy born of their special interdependence. Sustaining the community and what it stood for and perpetuating it through children and grandchildren was a way of life in the community. I can go back to my home community right now, and it still feels just like it did then. I see those children and grandchildren carrying on the same spirit of the community that was handed down to them.

Likewise, a strong business community can point to a history of effectiveness. Even if it's only been operating for a short time, any successful business community can show how it has intentionally put forth the effort to continually build on a strong foundation and put those reins into the hands of well-developed successors. The good news is it's never too late to start creating that strong foundation and good history!

One of the key ways the community legacy became self-sustaining was through what I call *legends*, and that's factor number nine. What I mean by legends are people who have lived in the community who embodied what the community was all about. Maybe they were some of the original settlers and founders of the community. Maybe they had been active in starting or growing the church. Maybe they played a large role in the school. Or perhaps it was some other reason entirely. But always, in a successful community, there are those individuals to whom people can point and about whom people can reminisce who helped make the community what it is today. I remember seeing old photographs hanging in the church and the school and the store of men with long beards and women wearing bonnets whom I never knew. But I knew they were important because I knew their stories.

Storytelling—that oral tradition that preceded the printing press—was alive and strong in the community where I grew up. The stories of our founding fathers and mothers, and the values of our community that they founded, were kept alive and perpetuated through those community legends. In this manner, they provided an ideal image—a role model—for everyone to seek to emulate. To be a part of the community and to take pride in one's role in the community was to aspire to the standards those legends of our community had established.

A community without legends lacks the important symbols of that for which it stands. It's like trying to define beauty. It may be very difficult to describe to someone what I find beautiful. But if I can point to a newborn baby and say, "That, to me, is beauty," then, you know what I mean, because you can see it. That's what we gain from these legends in the community. They teach us what our community means to us. They show us the way. When I think back to my own community, I remember several key people—some of them dead now—whose legend still continues to teach long after they're gone . . . and probably will continue to do so for years to come.

Leaders in the business community must be willing and able to become these symbols. They must walk the talk, because people are always watching. They must know what kind of community they want to build. They must be intentional about their efforts to build it. And they must be consistent. They will then become the legends and the symbols employees seek to emulate, and they will leave a legacy that no member of the organization wants to tarnish.

Those legends help give a community a common *language*, which is also very important in the community. Language is our final factor. Similar to what I was saying earlier about defining beauty, in a strong community there is a common understanding about what matters most. A good example would be the word *successful*. To be successful in one community might be entirely different than what is considered successful in another. In a farming community, success is defined in farming terms. But in a community located closer to town, for instance, daily life might revolve more around commerce, so the definition of success would be different.

A strong community has clarity about its desired results and the inherent meaning of the words and ideas used to describe the values and behaviors of the community. Members of the community know what is and is not acceptable behaviors with other members of the community—there is a common understanding. Through this common language people know what it "looks like" to be an effectively functioning member of the community. Any confusion about that is eliminated.

On a funny note, however, I will have to admit that in our community there was a humorous aspect of this common language, which I often joke about in my training. We had a tendency to just make up our own words. We not only had unique pronunciations of some words and names that defied the laws of the vocabulary, we also shortened, elongated, or twisted words around to sound the way we thought they should. These words eventually became the common dialect.

I love to tell stories and make people laugh using some of those words. It's no wonder I received some funny looks when I was working in Europe. I was in my late twenties before I actually corrected my pronunciation of some words and I still haven't corrected some of them! But the funny thing is, I can go back home today and use those words and no one would bat an eye. In fact, it would cause more of a shock if I actually pronounced them correctly.

What I learned about the importance of a common language in a community is that it doesn't matter what you say or how you say it; what matters is that everyone in the community knows what you mean and that it conveys the desired message.

Business communities must spend time getting very specific about what they're about and what they need from the members. They then need to do the right things to ensure everyone is speaking that language.

Wright

Rhonda, that's an amazing observation you have about building community, and I can see how important it would be to do that very thing in the workplace, but when you work with businesses and organizations, how do you translate this into something they can use?

Jones

It's simple. I may have learned all this in the community where I grew up, but it was in the business world where I actually figured out how to use and apply it. For many years I had been leading global projects, sometimes with team members from different countries whose native language I didn't even speak, before I finally realized that what I had actually been doing all that time—instinctively and intuitively—was building community. As the leader of my project teams, I had to determine our purpose, the unique knowledge, skills and abilities each team member could contribute, and the manner in which I could infuse the group with a spirit of pride for the project, create a common understanding—a common language—for what it meant for our project to be successful, and develop an environment of abundance, sharing, and helping that would empower each person to do what he or she did best.

I often used stories—examples and legends—to make our project team take on a life and culture of its own. As a result of that approach, I not only experienced personal success, but I was asked to help teach young management trainees how to engage in successful leadership. When I really started thinking about what it was I did and how I did it, in order to teach and mentor others, these common-sense ideas became very clear to me. I think they resonate with business and organizations because their profoundness lies in their simplicity. It isn't rocket science.

There's certainly nothing wrong with having a PhD, but you don't need a PhD to apply this approach to work and life. You just need to focus on these principles, be intentional about what you think, say, and do when you're attempting to live by them, and pay attention to and learn from the results you generate. That's how each individual grows their common sense, which is one of the keys to building and maintaining an effective community. Everything needs to make sense!

Wright

Yes, I wanted to come back to that. You said earlier that we could grow our common sense. What did you mean by that?

Jones

We hear about IQ—our intelligence quotient—and EQ—our emotional intelligence. But I think I may be the first to talk about our CSQ—our common sense quotient. If you study the human brain and psyche, and adult education or some related field dealing with human capability and development, you know there are actually many different types of intelligence. Without going into detail about that, I can tell you that they can all pretty much be lumped into one of the three categories I've just mentioned—IQ, EQ, or CSQ.

I personally believe that CSQ, much more than the other two, is not only the one we have the greatest possibility and probability of increasing, but it's also the one from which we stand to benefit the most in our lives. I could argue that CSQ is the only one of the three that is not essentially static.

Wright

How's that?

Jones

Well, as I said, there are many different theories about intelligence and the types of intelligence humans possess. There are also different theories about how to measure intelligence and the importance or lack thereof of those measurements. But one thing is fairly common across all those theories—at least to some degree, great or small depending on which theory you believe. It is possible not necessarily to increase but to *develop* your IQ and EQ.

Most theories suppose that, through education and training and exposure to new challenges, what you're actually doing is developing and utilizing more of the intelligence you already possessed innately. It's like saying you might be able to add a little sweetener to the coffee, but you can't put any more coffee in the cup. Common sense, however, is practical wisdom learned through everyday experiences. Every day that we live we have new experiences—new opportunities to learn and thereby *increase* our CSQ.

If I'm intentional about trying to learn from all those experiences and interactions with others, then my common sense cup will soon "runneth over"! That's how I learned all those key factors of community when I was growing up. I learned it from the continual stream of experiences I had in the community and as I now apply these principles, I continue to learn more every day. My CSQ is still growing!

What I do with companies and their employees is make them aware of the impact of these common principles for building community, and it's that awareness that really propels them on the road to success.

Wright

Some people have called you a female Andy Griffith, due to your down-to-earth approach and your use of stories and country humor to teach people about your common sense approach to building community. How do you feel about that?

Jones

It's funny you would mention that. I now consider it a huge compliment. The character Andy Griffith made famous in the sixties on the sitcom by the same name was wise and insightful without being arrogant or egotistical, and he certainly cared about people and understood and valued the importance of community. But I have to admit that I didn't always take it as a compliment. For many of the early years of my career, I worried that my simple, even backward, country background would be a liability rather than an asset. I think that's a big reason education was so important to me. I felt like I had to have those credentials in order to be accepted and respected.

Still, education didn't erase my country origins. It was still evident in many ways. For instance, I would cringe every time someone made a comment about my southern accent, and I would just about die when, in a foreign country, my dialect was confusing or unintelligible. I felt it was a negative stereotype held by the whole world that I had to overcome. Gradually, I began to realize it was only my youthful insecurities that caused me to feel that way about myself. No one else felt that way about me. On the contrary, they loved my stories and the fun we had together on my projects.

I realized that my country origins were also visible in a very positive way in the manner I did my work from which others could really learn a lot. I came to realize that everyone, regardless of where they grew up, has this image in his or her mind of that idyllic place—*the farm . . . the country*—where the sun always shines and the people are always friendly and helpful. Whenever they can be transported there, they are ready to go, whether it's through a funny or heartwarming story or through a project team that feels like an effective little community. Ultimately, I developed a liberating appreciation for my simple, country background when I started teaching others how to do what I do. I realized then that I really had learned everything I needed to know about effective living on the family farm in that little country community.

Wright

You sound very passionate about your theories and your work. It sounds like you're on a mission.

Jones

I am, David. I truly don't think I could be this passionate about it if it were not my calling. A very wise man once told me, "Rhonda, the way you'll know that you're doing what you're called to do is by how it's received and confirmed by the community."

As soon as I started teaching from my down-home perspective, the for-profit and non-profit business community quickly confirmed it. And the way it's been received has been overwhelming. I absolutely love to tell these true stories and see my audiences laugh and cry while learning these important lessons. The love and energy they give back to me not only confirms the effectiveness of my work, it sustains it. I have no doubt that this was what I was born and have lived to do with this phase of my life. And I think it shows in how much I enjoy connecting with my audiences, students, and teams.

Wright

Today we've been talking with Rhonda Jones. Her unique ability to engage people at all levels of an organization, her practical, down-to-earth approach, and her use of humor, wit, and true stories, make her a dynamic and entertaining trainer, speaker, and highly effective organizational consultant.

Thank you so much Rhonda for being with us today on *Mission Possible!*

About The Author

Raised on a farm in the countryside near Greeneville, Tennessee, Rhonda S. Jones has spent her entire adult life working with people and teams to bring about mutually beneficial outcomes. As a high school and college athlete in her youth and a project manager and director of corporate improvement programs in adulthood, Rhonda has learned firsthand the importance of building effective communities of people within which each individual has the opportunity to do what he or she does best. Whether she's facilitating the development of informative project reports, inspiring strategy descriptions or presenting compelling management addresses, Rhonda's practical methods and stories teach lessons that stem from her deep desire to see all people living and working peacefully and productively together.

Rhonda S. Jones
Bright Hope Training & Consulting Services
P.O. Box 50730
Knoxville, Tennessee 37950
Phone or Fax: 865.769.7510
For more information and to contact Rhonda via e-mail, go to:
www.rhondajones.us

Chapter 4

TONY MAGEE

THE INTERVIEW

David Wright (Wright)

Today we're talking with Tony Magee, MS, MBA, who is the founder and President of PlatinumStar® Life-Strategies, a Los Angeles based personal and professional development firm. Child of a single mother, raised in a Watts Housing Project, a "typical" poor black kid headed for a suffocating life marked by violence and poverty, and then the first African-American to earn a Master's Degree in Materials Science and Engineering from Lehigh University; then an MBA from Pepperdine University; then a scholar in Executive MBA Studies at Oxford University in England; then a high-end career in corporate America, professional awards, power and influence, wellbeing and happiness. Tony is a professional member of the National Speakers Association. He is the creator of the cutting-edge Destiny On Demand™ Home Study Course and celebrated author of several books including, *Can't Shove a Great Life into a Small Dream*, a top-selling uplifting book endorsed by the creators of *Chicken Soup for the Soul Series®*.

Tony Magee, welcome to *Mission Possible!*

Wright

How did you become "The Destiny Doctor™"?

Tony Magee (Magee)

As an African-American "man-child" growing up in South Central Los Angeles among gang violence, juvenile delinquency, academic underachievement, low teacher expectation, and high school drop-outs, I knew at a very young age that I wanted more out of life. I wanted a life greater than the one I had inherited. I didn't want to be held down by my unstable environment and background. I was too aware of what a dead end this could be. (For this I gotta thank my mother and grandmother.)

So I worked hard, got an education, and a couple of graduate degrees, thinking and knowing that this was what I needed—for the most part. And in so many ways this was right. But as I climbed the mountain of education and attainment, I began to realize an incredibly important fact: one's destiny isn't out there, ahead, in the fogbank of the next accomplishment. One's true Destiny was right here, immediate.

This is how Destiny On Demand™ was born. Before creating visions, goals, and game plans, demand this moment that you're already there. *Praise, enthusiasm,* and *gratitude* are the tools to fulfill one's destiny in an instant! Then go on and decide what you want to accomplish, how much money you want to make, what kind of car you want to drive, what kind of mansion you want, the color of your yacht, etc. If you do it in the reverse order, you may get to your goals, but you won't have fulfilled your destiny! (Folks, there are lot of unfulfilled, truly unhappy millionaires out there!)

Thus, I've been branded The Destiny Doctor™ to remind everyone—including myself—that we can all have a doctorate in life the minute we *choose* the power and magnificence of this exact moment!

Wright

Why do you consider yourself to be a "penny stock"?

Magee

By the beginning of the twelfth grade, I knew it was time to prepare for my freshman year in college. Applications were due and I had to get ready for my SATs. My grades were pretty good, but I didn't quite have all of the necessary course requirements to get into engineering school. Yes, I had completed all of the general subjects like history, government, English literature, physical education, earth science, and art. However, the highest level of math that I had studied was only geometry—not to mention that I had never taken any chemistry or physics. Nevertheless, my mind was set on going to college and somehow getting into engineering school.

To make this happen, I solicited help from three teachers at Westchester High. My goal was to train my brain to pass the college entrance exams. I've heard others say that *the teacher will appear when the student is ready*—boy was I ready! Mr. Brian Kataoka, my math teacher, trained me in math. Mr. Mario Tan, my science teacher, prepared me for chemistry and physics. Mrs. Margaret Bower, my art teacher, helped me improve my writing skills so I could pass the English placement portion of the exam. All of my college preparation occurred within six months before I was finally accepted at a university.

I had little money on my side, so I needed financial assistance for tuition, food, and housing. Luckily I was one of Mrs. Bower's favorite art students. She decided to invite me over for dinner one evening to meet her husband, Larry, and their four children, Justin, Erin, Ann, and Mary. The Bowers lived in Hermosa Beach, a suburban seaside community south of Los Angeles. Their beautiful home had an awesome view of the Pacific Ocean. It was as though *Ozzie and Harriet* had moved to *Fantasy Island*—certainly nothing I'd ever experienced. After a full course meal (which included broccoli fettuccini Alfredo, tossed salad, roasted Italian chicken, and homemade chocolate cake) my stomach was full and I was too happy. Mr. Bower took the time to review my college and financial aid applications to make sure everything was in order. Before the night was over, he said, *Margaret, I really like this kid. He's going to go far in life—really far. I say we adopt him.* And they did. They call me "Son" and we've been a family ever since 1986.

In college, two wonderful women sustained what my high school mentors had begun. These women went out of their way to continue to make things happen for me while I was attending California State University, Northridge (CSUN). Margaret June Brown was a well-known academic advisor who had looked out for my cousin Darryl Claiborne when he had attended CSUN a decade earlier. She kindly agreed to do the same for me. Ms. Brown helped me secure my course schedule, financial aid, and housing.

Gigi Littlejohn-McGuire was my other "shero" who served as a recruiter for the Minority Engineering Program at CSUN. Gigi strategically got me conditionally accepted into the School of Engineering for one year while I completed all of the prerequisites for full acceptance. She told me, "Tony, your positive attitude and enthusiasm for learning are more important in recruiting you than your transcripts. A lot of folks have the transcripts, but won't have the guts to finish the race. My bet is that you're not only going to finish, you're going to pass many at the grandstand. I believe in you!" In one year I made a quantum leap from geometry to calculus—from literally no real science to college chemistry and physics. My self-esteem was running on high.

Now, all I needed was a fine example to model myself after. I wanted a professor who would show me how to be an engineer—how to think, walk, talk, and dress like one. During my second year, it happened for me. Dr. Behzad Bavarian was not only my teacher, he became my mentor, friend, father figure, and lifetime advisor. Dr. B. would always say to me, *"Tony Magee, you will never be defeated!"* I believed anything he said. With his unconventional style of teaching, through the principles of discipline and preparedness, I found untapped excellence that would allow me to finish my undergraduate education and go on to earn two master degrees—one in engineering and the other in business. My relationship with Dr. Bavarian was like *Tuesdays With Morrie,* Mitch Albom's book about his relationship with his old college professor Morrie Schwartz.

Each one of the aforementioned people chose to help a challenged young person up out of his mud. They all invested their time and money in me. They recognized that *I was just like a penny stock*—an undervalued gem that would bring an excellent return on their investment!

Wright

While growing up surrounded by poverty and violence, what was the significant "turning point" in your life?

Magee

Surviving a very painful childhood and overcoming the enormous odds that were against me, I was determined to escape. In my mind, like Dorothy from *The Wizard of Oz*, who sang, if itty-bitty birds can fly high over the rainbow, why can't I? Somehow, I just needed to develop my wings.

December 17, 1986, was the day that changed my life forever. On this exciting day, I took my SAT exam to become one of the first in my family to go college. This would be a dream come true for everyone involved—especially my mother. On that same day, my mother—my earth who gave me life and many tidbits of wisdom unexpectedly—died of heart failure. I was just sixteen years old and devastated. What was I to do now? I realized I had a choice: was I going to become another negative ghetto statistic and succumb to the unstable situation that surrounded me, or was I going to raise myself up out of the mud of my wretched environment? Well, I didn't want to be stuck in the mud.

Wright

Tony, how did you go from the poverty and violence of the Nickerson Gardens Housing Projects in Watts to one day becoming an international scholar in business at Oxford University?

Magee

Looking back, I can see that the odds were against me. However, when I learned about my mother's death, I realized that I had to keep on going—that I could not enjoy the great life I wanted so badly with a small dream. My basic goal was to make my mama proud of me. I just wanted to make her smile up in heaven and say, "Now *that's* my baby right there!"

Today, whenever I think of my mother, the first thing that comes to my mind is the engraving on her tombstone. It simply reads:

Novel Jean Taplin-Magee
May 18, 1938–December 17, 1986

The first date is the day she entered into this world. The second date is the day she exited. The three children she had nurtured, the lives she touched, and all of the wonderful memories she created for us are all summarized by the hyphen between those two dates. Everything my mother ever accomplished—or didn't accomplish—is now an unassuming little dash. It seems, when its all said and done, life ends up being that tiny little dash between two dates engraved on a tombstone, and that tombstone sits on a graveyard plot that hardly anyone ever stops to visit.

What can we do to make our life an awesome life? What can we do to make our dash an awesome dash? Life just may be a little dash between our birth date and our death date, but we want to experience the best life possible, right? Right! The best thing we can do is to reduce our problems, prepare ourselves for the unforeseen, enjoy the good times, endure the bad times, and then handle whatever is expected.

Wright

What does it mean to get my "Destiny On Demand"?

Magee

DESTINY

"The 'Birthright'—the 'Master Plan'—the reason we're here on this planet at this time. A free and fulfilled life. A life of advantage. All of us have a future, because a future just happens to us. Few of us end up with a Destiny, because Destiny must be rigorously summoned." (From Magee's *"Tell-It-Like-It-Is" Dictionary*.)

DEMAND

"An act of asking with authority; something claimed as due; the requirement of work or of the expenditure of a resource."—*Webster's New Collegiate Dictionary*.

Tony Magee, MS, MBA—The Destiny Doctor™—states unequivocally that it is the destiny of the human being to have a truly amazing life—a life filled with abundance, love, success, health, and well-being. He also quickly adds that achieving one's destiny is not a casual undertaking. You have to "demand" it—first of yourself, then of your supporting cast.

Human beings are creatures of habit, and unless one's habits are truly pointed to the top of the mountain—destiny—you will not get there. You may make it part way, you may attain a "comfortable" life, but you won't fulfill your destiny.

It's as simple as that.

"Destiny On Demand™ helps you discover *where* you want to go and *how* to get there."—Tony Magee, MS, MBA

Wright

Who inspired you to "live your dreams out loud"?

Magee

Mattie Marie Taplin, born August 6, 1916, my "witty" grandmother is my number one "shero." She taught me the most valuable lesson of my life, "Baby, with a good education, your life's work will be as *light as a pen*; without it your life's work will be as *heavy as that spade*."

My grandmother (who we all called "Mama") loved to tell us stories of her childhood while growing-up on Big Daddy's farm in Clarksdale, Mississippi. Big Daddy, or "Papa" as she would affectionately call him, was Mama's father.

My grandmother had noticed just how much time kids were spending playing foolish games, running around outdoors, and some of the mischief we would get into. She would sometimes discourage me from wanting to play so much with my little knuckle-headed friends.

Mama loved telling us stories about how hard life was back on Big Daddy's farm. She told tales of how she and her siblings had to walk 150 miles to school, over a big hill, in the snow with no shoes. Then 150 miles back home just to help Big Daddy on his farm. No matter how fantastic the stories were she always made her point. There was always work to be done. In the summertime she said they would work on Papa's farm from *"can't see in the morning until can't see at night"* plowing the fields, picking vegetables and cotton, and milking those cows. They even made their own ice cream out of fresh snow no one had walked on.

But on this one particular hot day in 1978, while visiting Mama during my summer vacation it felt like the inside of an oven outside. My grandmother summoned me to come home from playing flag football in the street with my knuckle-headed friends to do some gardening work for her. When I got to the house we headed for the backyard. Mama asked me to dig a hole for her new rose bush. That day, it was hotter than any July in all of Africa, two Indias, and a Victorville. Mama said to me, "Baby, I want you to take that there spade [a shovel] and dig Mama a hole for this here rose bush." Using her hands to emphasize the dimensions, she said, "Dig Mama a hole this big-of-round and this here deep." She instructed me to dig the hole near an old brick-wall fence away from the rest of her garden, where Mama like to plant her turnip, collard, and mustard greens.

With my face dripping with dirty, salty sweat, I took the spade and began digging the hole. Mama went inside the house to fix us some lemonade and said she would be back to check on me. As the sweat drenched my clothes and the inside of my mouth felt like I just ate a lemon, my mind drifted. I thought I smelled Mama's good ol' southern fried chicken and hot water cornbread. Then I thought, "I'd give anything right now for a plate, but instead I have to dig this stupid hole." The time passed so slow, that with each beat of my heart it seemed like an eternity.

Thirty minutes went by, then an hour, then an hour and fifteen minutes. I had not even gone two inches past the top surface of the soil. Frustrated and thirsty I started getting mad at the dirt. I even kicked it a few times. I couldn't believe I was missing football to dig a hole in the ground. Finally, Mama returned to the backyard with a pitcher of ice-cold lemonade and two large jelly-jar glasses. She said, "You ain't finished diggin' Mama's hole yet, Baby? What's taking you so long?" I told her, "Mama this dirt is harder than steel."

Mama told me to take a break and have a glass of lemonade with her. I was happy 'cause it was burnin' hot and plus Mama made that good kind of lemonade. It would be so good and sugar-sweet that you'd have to take your shoes off so you could wiggle your toes—it was that Mississippi stuff. I gulped down my first two glasses in less than a minute. After wiping my face and mouth with my dirty shirt, I told Mama, "Sorry I couldn't dig the hole for you. I tried Mama. I even have blisters on my hands to prove it."

Her voice was filled with compassion as she told me the reason I could not dig a hole in that particular area was because there was a block of excess cement just beneath the surface of the dirt from that old brick fence. She said, "Baby, on the surface, the ground by that there fence looks the same as the rest of the yard. But ain't it funny how folk always say *'what you don't know won't hurt you?'* I want you to know what you don't know can *kill* you. You didn't know about that hidden chunk of concrete, now did you? Now tell me again, how do those blisters on your hands feel?"

Mama knew all along what she was doing. I was upset, but knowing Mama, she had a reason for it all. She was teaching me about life and education. She would sometimes discourage me from wanting to play so much with my little knuckle-headed friends. She said, "Children now-a-days play entirely too much and think they know everything. What they need to know is the value of hard work, and to spend more time preparing for their future. They need that down home kind of discipline. It takes a village to raise a little child, but if that village is crazy, then they will raise some very crazy kids. You are my grandchild and I want you to go to college some day and become more of yourself. I want you to have the best chance to live your best life. It's of great importance to me. You see, Mama didn't have all the great opportunities that you young folk take for granted today."

As a working farm girl from Clarksdale, Mississippi, my grandmother was only able to finish the ninth grade. Not because she wasn't bright, in fact she was one of the smartest pupils in all of her classes. Mama and her eleven brothers and sisters all had to lend their hands to labor Big Daddy's farm. She thought wisely to place an emphasis on the value of education for my life.

In retrospect, this event has become the most important defining moment of my life. I often ask myself where would I have been without my grandmother's wisdom and her belief in my becoming a major success.

Surviving the poverty and violence within the concrete-block walls of Watts Nickerson Gardens Housing Projects, earning a BS in Industrial Engineering, becoming the first African-American to receive a Master's degree in Material Science and Engineering from Lehigh University, earning an MBA from Pepperdine, completing Executive MBA studies at Oxford University in England, and enjoying a quality life turned out to be the easiest things I'd ever accomplished. The hardest thing was believing that I could. My grandmother knew it and surely believed it. That's why we must always thank God for those who believe in us when we sometimes don't believe in ourselves.

The moral of the story is this, as Mama would put it, "With education, you'll gain the knowledge and power to effectively communicate and use words constructively. You'll be able to enhance your life, change your game, add letters to your name, change your address and more importantly, change your bank account. Baby, with a good education your life's work will be as light as a pen. Without it your life's work will be as heavy as that spade."

Wright

What is one simple piece of advice you would offer to anyone who has had enough of feeling "stuffed into a bucket"?

Magee

Living well cannot be an accident. Your life must be on purpose; you must intend to do what you do. For instance, you must intend to be happy. If you don't intend to be happy, happiness will escape you. Happiness requires work—you have to work at it. You have to try to be happy.

Sometimes you need to reorganize your priorities in order to be happy. And certain things that make you unhappy should not be thought about. We must think ourselves into happiness.

Yes, living well will never happen by accident. A good marriage doesn't happen by accident. Good kids do not happen by accident. A good day doesn't happen by accident. You choose to make it a good day. It is totally up to you!

John Mason once said, "Your destiny is not a matter of chance—it is a matter of choice. Many people have the right aims in life, they just never get around to pulling the trigger."

Wright

What does it take for one to become a "Master of Life's Changes"? And what are the conditions of change?

Magee

In order to master something as seemingly unpredictable as change, you need to know the conditions of change, and before you can even begin to grasp their intricacies, you have to do the prep work. If you haven't done the prep work, when you're in the fray of the battle and have to go with the flow of change, you'll wilt like a daisy in the desert.

Prep Work for Change Mastery:

- *Take your blinders off*—See things for the way they really are.
- *Shatter excuses in your life*—Drop your convenient stories, and all the oh-so-dramatic reasons you can't get it together.
- *Upgrade your habits*—If your habits aren't going to lead you to your dreams, either downgrade your dreams or upgrade your habits.
- *Be grateful*—For you, for us, for everything, especially for the vicissitudes of life, you've got to love change to master it.

The payoff for mastering change is freedom. If you can flow with change, you're way ahead of the game. Most of us are hanging on for dear life, gripping the status quo so tightly that our knuckles are whiter than Granny's hair. Change mastery is directly linked to self-love and self-reliance. The more able we are to depend on ourselves, the more prepared we are for change. Self-esteem and self-respect are the most important prerequisites for the evolution of your life.

The following "Conditions of Change" will help you to know that you can master change in the same way that you've mastered other things in your life.

> "You are what your are and where you are because
> of what has gone into your mind,
> and you can change what you are
> and where you are
> by changing what goes into your mind."—*Zig Ziglar*

The Conditions of Change are:

Count your victories. When confronted with a big change in your life, take a moment to tote up your latest wins—big and small. This prepares you for the windstorm that often accompanies change.

Do what you love; love what you do. I know you've already heard this but it's a truism. If you're not doing what you really love to do, making a change—unless it's in the direction of your destiny—can feel like water torture.

Feelings first. Any change—especially major change—requires that we face the feelings and emotions that show up. If you're not willing to get in touch with your feelings and express them when appropriate, you're not going to master change. Period.

Give credit where credit is due. No matter what happens, if you have the courage to go through change, give yourself a blue ribbon for trying. Only the brave are willing to go up to the dragon of change and ask him for a kiss.

Love yourself, love yourself, love yourself. And while you're at it include *us* in your love nest. Self-love and respect is the ticket, whatever the show may be.

Risk, risk, risk. When a positive, albeit challenging change requires risk, don't hesitate. Leap! There is no safety net, and thank God, you don't need one! As my personal hero, the Dalai Lama says, "Great love and great achievements involve great risk."

Take the high road. When confronted with the choices that change brings, make the choice that conforms most with your values and ideals.

Trust your instincts. You—and you alone—know what's best for your life. Tune in, determine what feels right, and change will be exhilarating, not exhausting.

What's the worst thing that can happen? Write it down—create a solution-oriented contingency plan. If you're prepared for the worst thing that can happen, the reality is easier.

Being able to make changes gracefully requires that we know how to make choices, and unfortunately you don't get that in your education. Look around. The people you admire—the entrepreneurs, path-finders, pioneers, and celebrities—are masters of change. They know who's writing their life script, and they also know that half of the script is improvised. There is nothing more boring and demeaning than the status quo.

Mastering change has great payoffs: self knowledge, self respect, self confidence, and self-esteem, not to mention that mastering change is the shortcut to fulfilling your destiny.

The bottom line is freedom—you came to this planet with the blueprint of freedom and fulfillment. If you've been a change-phobic up until now, like anything worthwhile, mastering change is going to take practice. Experiment, take baby steps, be gentle with yourself, but know this: you are a master of change and it's about time that you knew it!

"Beliefs generate your thoughts and emotions, which create your experiences. To change your life, change your beliefs."—*Dick Sutphen*

Wright

What is the "4 S Life Cycle" and why is it so important for everyone to know?

Magee

In our lives, we all must deal with some level of the "4 S Life Cycle." You see, this represents four different levels of life situated in tiers like a four-step staircase that goes upward and downward depending on which direction one is headed in life.

Survival—When a mother gives birth to her newborn baby, usually there is enough pain involved to kill both of them. But 99 percent of the time, both the mother and child survive. When a person moves to a new neighborhood he or she isn't quite certain where the best post office or grocery store is located—which one has the best service than all of the rest. If you are the new person at work, school, or any other institution, you might not know exactly how to find your way around; you are in survival mode until you can elevate to the next level of life.

Stability—A person moves out of their parents' home into his or her own apartment. He or she may trade in his or her bus pass for the keys to a used but reliable Nissan Sentra to get around town. One is no longer unemployed, so he or she can afford to return the favor and take a friend to lunch for a change. Things are stable at the moment, however the next level of life is much more attractive.

Success—You trade in your keys from your apartment in for the keys to your new house. You trade in your Sentra for your dream car—a brand new S-Class Mercedes Benz. You received a major promotion at work or you have just graduated Magna Cum Laude from college. Whatever the accomplishment, things are looking up for you. Many believe that success is the ultimate goal in life, but it is not. It is merely a stepping-stone to the ultimate goal—your destiny, your best life, which is the ultimate level of life.

Significance—Significance is the snowcap of life's mountain. It is your destiny, your best life. People who are significant usually only go by one name. Can you say Oprah, Cher, Mother Theresa, Mandela, Lucy, Malcolm, Gandhi, Martin, and so on. If I said the name "Bill" you'd think Gates, Clinton, or Cosby. If I said the name "Michael," you'd think Jordan or Jackson (depending on what subject we're talking about), then you'd think Johnson or Tyson. We are here on earth to live and fulfill a truly amazing life of freedom and happiness, which is a life of significance.

Survival, Stability, Success, and *Significance* is the "4 S Cycle of Life," which is important for everyone to know.

Wright

What was the incentive to write your first book, *Can't Shove a Great Life into a Small Dream?*

Magee

As an American child, I was born to a single mom caring for two teenage kids. My mother had to drop out of high school in the eleventh grade due to certain hardships. She raised us amid the poverty and violence at the hardened Nickerson Gardens Housing Projects in the Watts neighborhood of Los Angeles. Facing these harsh conditions, what would the future hold for Tony Magee? My mother told me that I might've been born into poverty, but poverty was not born in me. She said that I was her son, a child of God, and that I was made out of some very special ingredients. My mom told me that I was special—I was bold, beautiful, black, and brilliant. At an early age, she convinced me that it was possible to obtain anything my eyes could see. She said, "Son, all it takes is hope and a good plan." All I ever wanted was a better life than the one I had inherited.

One might wonder how I managed to move upward. How did I go from the poverty and violence of the Nickerson Gardens Housing Projects in Watts to becoming an International Scholar in business at Oxford University in England?

Somehow I realized that I needed to learn these "Twelve Life Essentials" that would make my dream possible.

Wright

What are the "Twelve Life Essentials"?

Magee

As you move through the book, *Can't Shove a Great Life into a Small Dream*, you'll work through the Twelve Life Essentials; each one is the focus of a chapter in the book.

Life Essential No. 1: *Being Inspired for an Education*

In the first chapter you'll see that we acquire the skills of living successfully through knowledge. Knowledge when properly applied equals power—it is fundamental. If you think education is too expensive, then try ignorance!

Life Essential No. 2: *Defining Your Major Purpose in Life*

In Chapter Two you'll ask yourself, "What on Earth am I here for?" You'll learn the importance of finding and fulfilling your life's assignment. Your life purpose is directly linked to your true happiness.

Life Essential No. 3: *Developing Self-Esteem*

I'll show you how to raise your level of self-worth, self-respect, and self-confidence in Chapter Three. Self-esteem is the single most important quality of highly successful people. You'll see that all of what we know is not nearly as important as how we feel about ourselves!

Life Essential No. 4: *Navigating through Life's Changes*

The life-essential of Chapter Four will help you to embrace change versus fighting it. The only thing in life that's permanent is change.

Life Essential No. 5: *Choosing a Positive Attitude*

You are what you think about all day long. We have the power to choose whether today is going to be a good day or a lousy one. I'll show you why your attitude is your most valuable possession in Chapter Five.

Life Essential No. 6: *Setting Goals and Achieving Them*
The truth is that most of us don't have a problem achieving our goals; we have a problem setting them. Thus, you'll discover the importance of setting goals in order to achieve your dreams in Chapter Six.

Life Essential No. 7: *Having Financial Discipline*
In Chapter Seven, you'll learn that money is not the root of all evil, the lack of money is. All dreams have to be financed in some way. It's money that makes the world go 'round. A dream without money to back it will never become a reality.

Life Essential No. 8: *Becoming a Competent Leader*
In this chapter, you'll learn the traits of a leader and why clarity of vision for your dream is key.

Life Essential No. 9: *Influencing the World around You*
In Chapter Nine, you'll master the art of persuasion and come to understand why you should see yourself as a brand to be marketed to the world. No matter who you are, your talents are absolutely marketable.

Life Essential No. 10: *Creating Balance in Life*
This chapter presents simple ways to enjoy your life while making a living—to live for your passion and not your pension. You will learn to develop a style of living that creates balance and a sense of well-being in order to support who you are and where you are in every area of your life.

Life Essential No. 11: *It Takes a Team to Fulfill a Dream*
Is your life filled with diverse people who are committed to a common goal? You can't rise above mediocrity without learning how to use the minds of other people. This chapter's life-essential will demonstrate why fulfilling your dreams is not a project for one person.

Life Essential No. 12: *Great Readers Make Greater Leaders*
The last chapter offers my personal book list. Contained within this list may rest the unseen key, which when turned will unleash the power within you so you can live your dreams.

These profound strategies can deeply enhance the quality of your life! They've been the secrets to my success both personally and professionally. I suggest that you read the contents of *Can't Shove a Great Life into a Small Dream* as though you and I are personal friends and I'm writing to you and only you.

Wright

As an author, what is your advice to those who feel they have a book "waiting to come out of them"?

Magee

Never be afraid to go out on a limb 'cause that's where the very best fruit lies! Everyone has an award-winning story to tell and thousands upon thousands of others are indeed interested. Someone once asked, "Tony how did you write your book and make it seem so easy?" I responded kindly, by saying, "One page at a time with a well thought-out outline that I followed!"

People should embrace their creativity! I thought like Alan Alda who said, "Be brave enough to live life creatively. The creative is the place where no one else has ever been. You have to leave the city of your comfort and go into the wilderness of your intuition. You can't get there by bus, only by hard work and risk and not quite knowing what you're doing. What you'll discover will be wonderful. What you'll discover will be yourself." So start writing your bestseller today—one page at a time!

About the Author

TONY MAGEE, MS, MBA, is the founder and President of PlatinumStar®
Life-Strategies, a Los Angeles based personal and professional development
firm. Child of a single mother, Tony was raised in a Watts Housing Project, a
"typical" poor black kid headed for a suffocating life marked by violence and
poverty, and then became the first African-American to earn a Master's Degree in Materials Science and Engineering from Lehigh University, then an
MBA from Pepperdine University. He then became a scholar in Executive
MBA Studies at Oxford University in England, then had a high-end career in
corporate America. He gained professional awards, power, influence, well-
being, and happiness. Tony is a professional member of the National Speakers Association. He is the creator of the dynamic Destiny On Demand™ Home
Study Course and celebrated author of several books including, *Can't Shove a
Great Life into a Small Dream*, a top-selling uplifting book endorsed by the
creators of *Chicken Soup for the Soul Series*®.

Tony Magee, MS, MBA – The Destiny Doctor™
PlatinumStar® Life-Strategies
P.O. Box 891
Woodland Hills, CA 91365
Phone: 1.866.ASK.TONY (1.866.275.8669)
E-mail: tony@platinumstar.com
www.platinumstar.com

Chapter 5

VALARIE EILAND DAVIS

David Wright (Wright)

Today we are talking with Valarie Eiland Davis. Valarie is the founder of Venterprises, LLC, a Performance Improvement Consultancy. She describes herself as a "human compass" who uses coaching, training, planning, and problem-solving to help her clients discover their purpose and travel the right paths to achieve their goals.

Ms. Davis served as Director of Strategic Planning at Fannie Mae and held management positions with Proctor & Gamble and Ernst & Young. Her education includes a Juris Doctor degree from Georgetown University Law Center, a Master of Business Administration degree in marketing from the University of Michigan, and a Bachelor of Science degree in finance from Boston University. She is also a trained coach at the Mastery Level. She has won numerous awards including Outstanding Young Woman of America.

Valarie, welcome to *Mission Possible!*

Valarie Eiland Davis (Davis)

Thank you.

Wright

What an impressive educational resume.

Davis

Many of my educational accomplishments are due to my parents—I have to give credit where credit is due. The latter half of my education is more a result of my making up my mind about what I wanted to do with my life.

Wright

You've made it your life's work to help individuals and organizations find their purpose and achieve their goals. Why is this so important to you?

Davis

It's important to me because I think it's important to most people. If you think about it, as adults we ask children from the time they can talk, "What do you want to be when you grow up?"

Even as adults we jokingly preface our discussions about what we want to do with our lives by saying, "When I grow up I'll____." So, I believe that every person on the planet is thinking about this consciously or subconsciously. I think each of us is designed to do something unique that no one else can do. I believe it's our life's challenge to figure out what that is and get on with it.

I really hate to see people struggling to fit themselves into jobs, relationships, homes, or even clothes that don't fit. Somehow they've reached a certain place in life and it's easier to stay there than to figure out what they were really created to do.

I want to see each person live out his or her purpose and I want to see it sooner rather than later.

Wright

What is your perspective on the way that most people approach the goals they want to achieve in their lives?

Davis

Unfortunately I think that most of us fall victim to what I call the "tyranny of the shoulds." We design and make decisions about our lives based on what we and other people think we *should* be doing. We take the job we think we should take. We major in the areas that people think we should major in. We even marry people others think we should marry, or live in places where others or we think we should live.

People don't spend significant time defining and setting their personal goals and then mapping out a plan to achieve those goals. The closest most of us get is deciding which job to take. That is really a very poor substitute for doing real, conscious, well thought-out introspection and planning. As a result, the decision about the first job we take sets a direction for the rest of our lives. Since we spend more of our waking hours working than doing anything else, that choice pretty much determines what our life is going to be like. We get on a certain career track and it becomes very difficult to make a change. It's even more difficult to reverse course in a major way and consider that we might have made some of the wrong decisions or decisions that are not consistent with our true purpose.

Here's an example. Let's say there is a young man who graduates from high school and he's thinking about going to college. He's fortunate because he's been offered a scholarship to a major college in his local area. But he has to major in engineering in order to get the scholarship. He has also been accepted into other colleges, and at those colleges he has the opportunity to become a veterinarian, which is what he has always wanted to do. The bad news is that neither he nor his parents can afford to pay his tuition to any of those other schools. Finances end up dictating his decision, not only which school he's going to attend but also the career options he's going to have.

He ends up attending the local college and majoring in engineering. But he suffers through the classes, getting average to good grades. He ends up working at a good firm making a good salary. He also has great benefits. But he's not doing what he wants to do.

On the one hand, he was blessed to get a college education. But he is unlikely to ever change course and decide to become a veterinarian. No one *planned* for him to become a veterinarian and it's no surprise that it didn't happen. That's what many of us do—let circumstances define our lives rather than planning to pursue our purpose.

Wright

How did you set your personal goals and why do you think you were able to achieve them?

Davis

The first time I remember actually setting goals for myself was in graduate school. I had finished my undergraduate degree at Boston

University and decided that I needed a graduate degree. That was the first time I put any effort toward figuring out what I wanted to do.

Prior to that my parents were the driving force behind anything I achieved. They made it very clear what the foundation of our lives as children would be. That was our faith, our family, excellence in education, and a very high degree of personal responsibility. I still run my life that way.

After I graduated from Boston University with a finance degree and had done everything I thought I should do, I received several job offers. I then found myself asking the question, "What exactly is it that I want to do?" I had done the things I thought I should have done and that I had prepared to do. I could work and support myself. Nobody needed to worry about whether I would survive and prosper. But I hadn't yet figured out what I really *wanted* to do and where I would fit.

During the last semester of college I actually spent time writing some things down. I thought about what I might like to do. I had never asked myself that question before. What I found out was that I didn't like finance. I knew I could get a good job in that area and I had received a full scholarship that allowed me to major in finance. But I had not thought about whether I *wanted* to work in finance as a career.

After I listed all the things I was good at doing and liked to do, I decided I wanted to work in marketing. I then went about the process of finding out what kinds of jobs involve marketing and what I needed to do to get those jobs and make the kind of money I thought I should make. I picked the job I wanted and I looked at the people who were in that field and the various backgrounds they had. I found out that, in order to make the kind of money I desired in marketing, I had to get a graduate degree—something that was definitely not on my agenda. I just knew I was through with school. I'd had enough of the classroom. But to get where I wanted to go I had to get an MBA degree, and that's what I did.

That was the first time I got organized and self-directed about setting a goal for myself, figuring out how to get there, and then making the decision to do it. It might not sound like a big deal now, but changing from finance to marketing and convincing people I was serious about it was pretty challenging because I had no education or work experience in marketing. It sounded to employers like I was wishy-washy and didn't really know what I wanted to do. But this time I actually did.

I think that for me the key was: (1) I believed that I could do what I wanted to do if I just figured it out; (2) I knew myself and figured out what I was good at doing (and what I was *not* so good at doing); and, (3) I realized I couldn't reach my career goal by myself. I could have gone out in the workplace after college and decided not to get the degree, but I don't believe that I would have been as successful. I realized I needed something from somebody else to get where I needed to go.

Wright

Should everyone be involved in striving to reach specific goals? What about those folks who feel truly content with their lives?

Davis

The fact is that everyone is involved at some level in striving to reach goals. Even if a person is content with his or her life just the way it is, their goal is to maintain that level of contentment. It is not a question of whether they *should* be involved, but it's more the realization that everyone is already involved in pursuing goals.

Wright

Isn't it the case that some people are naturally "goal-oriented" and others are not? Isn't it really a personality trait?

Davis

Not so. Everyone has goals. Some people may be more ambitious than others. Some people may be more driven than others. For me the difference is that the size, the magnitude, and the pace of their goal orientation are greater or faster than someone else's. The difference is not the presence or absence of goals.

Think, for example, about the classic race between the tortoise and the hare. The tortoise was slow but steady and the hare was quick and speedy. The fact is that both of them were in the race and both of them eventually crossed the finish line. So being one or the other in terms of fulfilling our goals is just a matter of choice. The choice is *how* to run the race not whether or not you're in it to begin with. I think everyone, consciously or sub-consciously, is oriented toward achieving something significant and special in life.

Wright

What is your advice for people who have tried unsuccessfully to reach personal and professional goals—those whose missions seem *im*possible?

Davis

My first piece of advice would be to *get the story right in your head*—get your mind right about what you're trying to do. If you're a person who is in that position, you've had some disappointments and you may have gone so far as to label yourself and your experiences as "failures." The first order of business is to shift your thinking away from failure to success. That's got to happen, because the only way you're going to stay in the game is if you think there is some hope and new possibilities. If you are already playing a tape in your head that says, "I'm a failure; I can't do it," that's exactly what your situation is and will be. You have to turn that tape off and turn on another one that says, "It hasn't worked out so far but I'm still in the race."

My second piece of advice is probably the most important and that is to *revisit the goal or objective you had at the beginning*. Is your goal under the tyranny of the shoulds—someone made you feel like you should do this or you think that you should? Is it really your own goal? If you look at your goals and imagine yourself achieving them, will it have a positive impact on your life? Is it going to get you where you want to go? Are your goals consistent with what you believe? Do people who are important to you actually support you in achieving your goals? Ask those critical questions about your goals and make sure they are the right goals in the first place. If you have tried and tried sincerely and put some effort toward achieving a goal and it has not worked, you definitely have to do a self-check to find out if you are even moving toward the right goal. The good news about trying and failing is that you have a lot of experience from which you can learn. You can learn from those experiences and move on without repeating the same mistakes.

The third piece of advice I have is probably the hardest for anyone to follow. I think it's where most of us miss the boat. My advice is to *get disciplined*.

If you study people we see as successful, you might be surprised to find that many of their successes are wonderful accidents. They have achieved great things but many might not be able to tell you why or how. It's okay to be clueless about your success formula as long as it's working. When your formula stops working and you don't know how it worked or what to fix, then you are in worse shape than someone who has never tried to succeed.

It's important to know how and why you have been successful as well as how and why you have not been successful. Take a good, hard look at every attempt you've made. Be critical. Be hard on yourself. Find out what works, change what isn't working, and figure out if there's some roadblock that keeps showing up over and over again.

I have one of those recurring roadblocks. My roadblock is that I fear failure. Letting someone else down is my version of failure—disappointing someone who is expecting something of me, whether it's a client, professor, neighbor, friend, or family member. It's not just that I don't like to fail, but the thought of it actually paralyzes me on the road to my goals and keeps me from making progress. Every time I'm trying to do something that I've never done before, that fear rears its ugly head. But because I know this is a potential roadblock for me I have developed a "tape" of self-talk to play in my head that boosts my confidence and reminds me that the worst that can happen won't be fatal or tragic. That affirmation gets me around the roadblock.

When you take this last step and institute some discipline in your goal work, you have to be just as critical as your mother would be if you asked her for constructive criticism or as if you were paying some high-priced executive coach to give you advice. After all, it's your *life* we're talking about. *You* must demand the highest possible level of success from yourself because the rest of the world is perfectly content to let you remain at status quo. *You* are the one who wants to make the change, so *you* are the one who needs to apply a critical eye to what you have done so far in your life.

Wright

What is the "discipline of achievement" and how can it help people achieve their goals?

Davis

As I suggested before, I believe that at some level we are all very curious about people who are successful and who have actually won their battles, achieved their goals, or produced their success. As a society we seem to be on a continual search to discover those illusive keys to success by examining the lives of the successful and not-so-successful in exposé books, magazines, and reality television shows. We seem to believe that if we watch people in their most vulnerable day-to-day moments we will figure out how they became who they are and discover the secrets of their success.

I think many of us would like to believe that extraordinary success is determined by factors beyond our control. We tell ourselves that, unlike the super-successful people, "I wasn't born with that talent. I didn't have the support of a wealthy family. I couldn't go to the best schools. My health has not been the best." We would like to think that the building blocks of great success are out of our reach because it gets us off the hook for pursuing similar success.

The reality is that when you really talk to high achievers who have thought about their success formulas at all, success is, more than anything, a function of personal discipline—even more than innate talent. Reaching success for them was rarely glamorous or quick. Like them, we have to be consistent and we have to have a well-conceived plan with clear goals and enough flexibility to cope with the things that happen in everyday life. That is what I would describe as the discipline of achievement.

Wright

Many people feel they don't have the time or especially the money to invest in trying to make their dreams come true. Aren't these true, legitimate reasons why so many people are not able to turn their dreams into reality?

Davis

I would agree with you that lack of time and lack of money are the two most frequent excuses for not achieving goals. I am deliberately choosing the word "excuses." Without exception, I have found these are never the true barriers. They are just the excuses that are the easiest to grab and generate the most sympathy from others. It is true that time is finite and that personal funds may be limited. But those are circumstances, not absolute barriers. At worst they are short-term constraints on the method or the pace at which you achieve your goals—not true barriers.

Let's look at a typical example based on my experiences as a coach. "Mystery Mom" is a married woman and the mother of two young children in elementary school. In her fondest dream, she wants to become an author of mystery novels. Here is the problem: She and her husband both work and it takes both their current salaries to pay the bills and save enough for a college education for their children. They have already run the numbers and a single income just won't suffice.

They are chugging along toward their goals but in her heart of hearts she knows what she really wants to do. Here is what she tells herself: "If we had more money I could quit work and write full time. But even if I had more money I would still need more hours in the day so I could have time to write my novel and still take care of my family." Time and money seem to be insurmountable barriers. On the surface those excuses sound reasonable and right.

But let's dig a bit deeper using one of my tried-and-true coaching challenges—the question "Why?" I would say to my client, "Talk to me about what is keeping you from achieving your goal of becoming a mystery novel writer." When she responds with her perceived barriers of money and time, I would ask her, "Why?" She would probably tell me that she cannot take the time to write at the risk of losing her salary, and I would again ask her, "Why?" She would probably tell me that she would not be able to make as much money writing as she would at her current job. I would again ask her, "Why is that?" In order to respond appropriately she would have to be able to compare her current salary with her expected earnings as a successful mystery novelist. She would not be able to do this because she would not have done the research to estimate her potential earnings if she were a best-selling mystery novelist. She could only make poor assumptions.

This is an example of what I mean by making excuses that keep us from achieving. There are always "red herrings" that are not really barriers to avoid but circumstances to be addressed. I'll bet if you asked many of the successful mystery novelists whose books Mystery Mom is reading how much money they are making, it would dwarf the income she currently earns. Furthermore, she might be surprised to learn that the majority of successful writers began their writing careers while working other jobs and managing their households. Mystery Mom has not invested the time to validate her barrier or prove it. She is probably very comfortable with her assumptions—excuses—because she will never have to make a move in the direction of her dreams. Her excuses are very convenient, aren't they? But the fact is, success is rarely convenient.

The perceived roadblocks of money and time, in my experience, are almost never the real barriers to achieving our goals.

Wright

In your experience as a career coach, what are the most common barriers that keep people from accomplishing their goals and how can they be overcome?

Davis

There are two very real barriers that frequently emerge. The first is fear and the second is lack of discipline. I alluded to these earlier.

Fear takes many forms. It can be fear of the unknown, which produces thinking that says, "I know what will happen if I stay where I am, but I just don't know what's going to happen if I make a change." Perhaps the fear is like mine, fear of failure. I don't want to let other people down. I just can't imagine being asked by someone who is depending on me why something didn't go as they expected. The potential for embarrassment and disappointment in myself can be paralyzing. There are even people who fear success because they don't know how they will handle it. They prefer to remain where they are because they have become comfortable with the limits of their current level of success and they cannot imagine what life would be like if they achieved their personal goals. Concerns dominate their thoughts rather than positive possibilities. They think, "What would it do to my family? Would it change who I am? Would I have to move somewhere else? Would I have to keep out-doing myself in order to meet other people's expectations? Would I have to make new friends?"

The second barrier is lack of discipline. Too often people just fail to do their homework when it comes to planning their own lives. We spend more time researching how to buy our next car than we do about what to do with our lives and what goals we want to achieve. Some people spend more time choosing a shampoo or dishwashing detergent than they do sitting with their children helping them figure out what they are good at doing and what they were born to do. Goal work takes discipline because it's not something that is done every day and no one else is going to require it of you. *This is your life.* Do your homework.

Another area of lack of discipline is having a "lone ranger" mentality. This occurs when we believe we can do it alone—we don't believe we need, nor do we want any help. Some people are afraid of help and cannot seem to feel good when others help them. In truth, it takes a self-aware and confident person to know when he or she needs the help of others and get it. It is undisciplined to think you can do everything on your own, especially big, bold accomplishments. Just think for a moment about the most important or major accomplishments of your life. Did you accomplish any of them as a "lone ranger"? I doubt it.

Lastly, lack of discipline occurs in the sense that people lose sight of what the ultimate payoff would be if they did what they were born to do. Mystery Mom cannot spend precious time every day—in-between washing the kids' clothes for the next soccer game, taking care of her husband, and remembering to take something out of the freezer for dinner, all after a ten-hour day at work—daydreaming about just how good life would be if she became a successful writer. But the fact remains that if she were to actually make a change and become a mystery novelist she would love her life so much more.

You know what they say, "If Mom's not happy, no one is happy." It follows that, if Mom's happy, everybody is happy. Pursuing her dreams would show her children that she and they can decide to do something different and wonderful with their lives. She would also be a happier wife if she were doing what she loves to do. These are huge payoffs. But it is much too easy to lose sight of the payoff of big dreams when we are all just trying to get by day-to-day. It takes great discipline to keep our goals and their payoffs in sight while we are still on the path to making them a reality.

Wright

Let's put your coaching skills to the test. What can a reader do within the next twenty minutes after reading this chapter to make real progress toward accomplishing their most important goal?

Davis

If our readers already have a goal in mind, they are far ahead of most folks. There are three simple steps to jumpstarting goal work. The steps are simple but they are not necessarily easy.

Step One: Set Your Goal.

This step has two parts:

A. ***Confirm your goal and establish an aggressive but realistic deadline.*** An example of a well-written goal statement might be: "I want to start a twenty-four-hour children's daycare center by January of next year." The goal is very specific. You are making a choice to start a daycare center —not buy it. You know your target market—people who would need a twenty-four-hour daycare with non-standard hours, such as doctors and nurses who work the night shift. Finally, you are setting a deadline of January of next year.

B. ***Understand the payoff.*** Complete two sentences:
   (1) I am pursuing this goal because _____.
   (2) When my goal is accomplished, my life will be enhanced because _____.
   (3) If you find yourself using the word "should" or writing only about the benefits to other people—your parents, your children, your spouse, your coworkers, your clients—then rewrite the goal and the payoff to make them personal to you.

Those are the two things you do to confirm that the goal you have chosen is one you are willing to sacrifice to accomplish—a goal that gets you excited and keeps you moving forward despite obstacles and excuses.

Step Two: Take a Personal Inventory

Create a list of the things you have and those you need to achieve your goal—your "haves and have-nots." Make a written list down the left side of a few pieces of paper of all the resources you could possibly need to accomplish your goal. Randomly list the people you need, the supplies, the education, the technology, the legal assistance, the facilities, etc. Do not try to organize the list, just make it as exhaustive as possible so that if you had everything on the list there would be no reason why that daycare center, for example, could not be started.

On the right side of your paper make three columns. Title the first column "Have," the second column "Have Not," and the third column

"Critical." Go down your list of resources and make a check mark next to each item in the Have column if you already possess the resource and you would not have to do anything to get it. For example, if I were going to be a daycare provider I would not be able to work from my home—I would need a separate space. If someone has already given me a lease to a building or I own a building I can use, I would put a check mark in the Have column by that need. If I didn't have a facility I would put a check mark in the Have Not column. If you have a portion of a resource but not all of it or if you are not sure you have it, then check the Have Not column. Don't cheat—you either have it or you don't.

Review your entire list. Now put up to ten checks in the Critical column next to the ten most immediate, important resource requirements for you to be able to make your goal a reality. One of the things most of us need is the support of the person(s) we spend the most time with, the person on whom we depend, or the person who depends on us. Often that is a spouse. For example, Mystery Mom really needs her husband's support to pursue her goal and if she has never mentioned it to him, that's a check in the Have Not column. It also requires a check in the Critical column. She must figure out a way to help him understand her goals and negotiate how the necessary changes are going to fit into their family life. Only then can she put a check mark in the Have column.

This brings me to a very important and sensitive issue.

Many of us would love to be able to assume that the people we care about the most will automatically support what we want to do. The biggest surprise you can have when you try to take a major step forward in a different direction is that the people who are closest to you, who depend on you, and who love you the most are often the most resistant. Fear for your well-being might show up from them as resistance. Your loved ones just want you to be successful; they don't want you to fail or be hurt. They also like the way you are now and may be startled by new changes in you. So don't *assume* you have their support. You need their support as a resource, so do the work to get it. Realize that you have just started something new and different that you have been thinking about and you are now ready to move forward. Everybody else in your life has to understand your new vision and decide if they are coming with you. It is your job to enroll those who are willing.

Step Three: Move Forward with Discipline

You know your goal and you know your deadline. You have an action item list with your ten most critical needs. Now you need a work plan. You need to make an assessment of how much time you need to spend every week working on your goals in order to meet your deadline. This is the most difficult part of the entire process because it involves change.

Decide what your workweek looks like for your new goal. If your life is as full as most people's lives are, you don't have too many extra hours (spent daydreaming or watching television) to devote to your new goal work. The time you now need to spend on this very important goal has to come from something you are currently doing even though everything important in your life must keep functioning. You need to negotiate with family members, friends, and whoever is going to be affected by this goal work to determine the functions that must be kept going that you can no longer perform. You need to determine who is going to assume those responsibilities, which functions are no longer necessary, and how everyone can work together to be supportive of your new goal.

Set your start date, mark your calendar, and then start working. Be disciplined—do not let anybody interrupt you. If you have set aside from five until six in the morning to work on your goal, then no one must disturb that time. If you decide that you are going to spend a half hour of every lunch break making phone calls and doing research, reading, and gathering information to reach your goal, then a half hour of every lunch break must be routinely devoted to those activities.

Goal work can be very lonely. As part of your discipline, find somebody who is going to be there for you, not just as a cheerleader but also as an accountability partner. This should be a person who will say, "Now wait a minute, you said you slept late the past few days. I thought you set aside from five to six in the morning to work on your goal. Let's get back on track starting tomorrow. How can I help?" Identify someone who will remind you of your promise to yourself—someone who will stay aware of your progress. It need not be someone you see all the time; maybe it's someone from your sorority, school, gym, or church. (This person is not likely to be a family member—keep those relationships less engaged.) It will be someone who can truly say they want you to reach your goal as much as you want to reach it and will be strong enough to tell you if you get off track.

Wright

What a great conversation. I really appreciate your spending all this time today to answer all these questions. I've learned a lot and I'm certain our readers will.

Davis

Thank you for the opportunity.

Wright

Today we've been talking with Valarie Eiland Davis who is the founder of Venterprises, LLC, a Performance Improvement Consultancy. As we have found, her description of herself as a human compass is one that is accurate. She uses coaching, training, planning, and problem-solving to help folks like us discover and travel the right paths to achieve the right kinds of goals.

Thank you so much Valarie for being with us today on *Mission Possible!*

About the Author

VALARIE EILAND DAVIS is the Chief Executive Officer of Venterprises, LLC, a company built to deliver on her passion for helping people discover and live out their divine purpose. Ms. Davis believes that God has created each of us for a unique purpose, and she is devoted to helping people realize their dreams and possibilities. Ms. Davis assists her clients in clarifying their goals and taking action to achieve them.

Ms. Davis's professional experience includes positions with Fannie Mae, Procter & Gamble, Howard University, and Ernst & Young. As an entrepreneur she led The Maxxis Group, a wealth creation company that coached start-up businesses; was co-founder of MIND*WELL*, LLC, a financial education provider; and was a founding partner of two equity investment partnerships.

Venterprises, LLC Consulting Group provides coaching and problem-solving services to clients seeking to make radical changes in new directions. The company's Realty Group helps clients achieve the American dream of home ownership by providing real estate services and financial education, as well as making direct property investments.

Ms. Davis is an inspiring professional speaker, trainer, and facilitator, and has won numerous awards, including *Outstanding Young Woman of America.*

Her educational achievements include a Bachelor of Science degree in finance from Boston University, a Master of Business Administration degree with a concentration in marketing from The University of Michigan, and a law degree from Georgetown University Law Center. She has trained as a Coach for several years, including training at the Mastery level.

Anthony and Valarie Davis reside in a wonderful Victorian home in Baltimore, Maryland, that they like to call "Green Acres," and they are members of the Temple of Praise in southeast Washington, D.C. They are blessed to be able to spend time with their friends and immediate family in the Washington, D.C. area as well as their extended family all over the country from California to Mississippi to New York. God has been very good to them and they work daily to be a blessing to others, including you.

Valarie Eiland Davis, Chief Executive Officer
Venterprises, LLC
2912 Gibbons Avenue
Baltimore, Maryland 21214
Phone: 443.320.1591
E-mail: venterprisesconsulting@comcast.net
valarie@venterprisesrealtygroup.com
www.venterprisesrealtygroup.com

Chapter 6

BRIAN TRACY

THE INTERVIEW

David Wright (Wright)

Many years ago, Brian Tracy started off on a lifelong search for the secrets of success in life and business. He studied, researched, traveled, worked, and taught for more than thirty years. In 1981, he began to share his discoveries in talks and seminars, and eventually in books, audios and video-based courses.

The greatest secret of success he learned is this: "There are no secrets of success." There are instead timeless truths and principles that have to be rediscovered, relearned, and practiced by each person. Brian's gift is synthesis—the ability to take large numbers of ideas from many sources and combine them into highly practical, enjoyable, and immediately usable forms that people can take and apply quickly to improve their life and work. Brian has brought together the best ideas, methods, and techniques from thousands of books, hundreds of courses, and experience working with individuals and organizations of every kind in the U.S., Canada, and worldwide.

Today, I have asked Brian to discuss his latest book, Victory!: Applying the Military Principals of Strategy for Success in Business and Personal Life.

Brian Tracy, welcome to *Mission Possible!*

Tracy

Thank you, David. It's a pleasure to be here.

Wright

Let's talk about your new book the *Victory! Applying* the *Military Principals* of *Strategy* for *Success* in *Business* and *Personal Life.* (By the way it is refreshing to hear someone say something good about the successes of the military.) Why do you think the military is so successful?

Tracy

Well, the military is based on very serious thought. The American military is the most respected institution in America. Unless you're a left liberal limp-wristed pinko most people in America really respect the military because it keeps America free. People who join the military give up most of their lives—twenty to thirty years—in sacrifice to be prepared to guard our freedoms. And if you ask around the world what it is that America stands for, it stands for individual freedom, liberty, democracy, freedom, and opportunity that is only secured in a challenging world—a dangerous world—by your military.

Now the other thing is, the people in our military are not perfect because there is no human institution made up of human beings that is perfect—there are no perfect people. The cost of mistakes in military terms is death; therefore, people in the military are extraordinarily serious about what they do. They are constantly looking for ways to do what they do better and better and better to reduce the likelihood of losing a single person.

We in America place extraordinary value on individual human life. That is why you will see millions of dollars spent to save a life, whether for an accident victim or Siamese twins from South America, because that's part of our culture. The military has that same culture.

I was just reading today about the RQ-1 "Predator" drone planes (Unmanned Aerial Vehicles—UAVs) that have been used in reconnaissance over the no-fly zones in Iraq. These planes fly back and forth constantly gathering information from the ground. They can also carry remote-controlled weapons. According to www.globalsecurity.org, the planes cost $4.5 million each and get shot down on a regular basis. However, the military is willing to invest hundreds of millions of dollars to develop these planes, and lose them to save the life of a pilot, because pilots are so precious—human life is precious. In the military everything is calculated right down to the tinniest detail because it's the smallest details that can cost lives. That is why the military is so successful—they are so meticulous about planning.

A salesperson can go out and make a call; if it doesn't work that's fine—he or she can make another sales call. Professional soldiers can go out on an operation and if it's not successful they're dead and maybe everybody in the squad is dead as well. There is no margin for error in the military; that's why they do it so well. This is also why the military principals of strategy that I talk about in *Victory!* are so incredibly important because a person who really understands those principals and strategies sees how to do things vastly better with far lower probability of failure than the average person.

Wright

In the promotion on *Victory!* you affirm that it is very important to set clear attainable goals and objectives. Does that theme carry out through all of your presentations and all of your books?

Tracy

Yes. Over and over again the theme reiterates that you can't hit a target you can't see—you shouldn't get into your car unless you know where you are going. More people spend more time planning a picnic than they spend planning their careers.

I'll give you an example. A very successful woman who is in her fifties now wrote down a plan when she was attending university. Her plan was for the first ten years she would work for a Fortune 500 corporation, really learn the business, and learn how to function at high levels. For the second ten years of her career she talked about getting married and having children at the same time. For that second ten years she would also work for a medium sized company helping it grow and succeed. For the third ten years (between the ages of forty and fifty), she would start her own company based on her knowledge of both businesses. She would then build that into a successful company. Her last ten years she would be chief executive officer of a major corporation and retire financially independent at the age of sixty. At age fifty-eight she would have hit every single target. People would say, "Boy, you sure are lucky." No, it wouldn't be luck. From the time she was seventeen she was absolutely crystal clear about what she was going to do with her career and what she was going to do with her life, and she hit all of her targets.

Wright

In a time where companies, both large and small, take a look at their competition and basically try to copy everything they do, it was really interesting to read in *Victory!* that you suggest taking vigorous offensive action to get the best results. What do you mean by "vigorous offensive action"?

Tracy

Well, see, that's another thing. When you come back to talking about probabilities—and this is really important—you see successful people try more things. And if you wanted to just end the interview right now and ask, "What piece of advice would you give to our listeners?" I would say, "Try more things." The reason I would say that is because if you try more things, the probability is that you will hit your target

For example, here's an analogy I use. Imagine that you go into a room and there is a dartboard against the far wall. Now imagine that you are drunk and you have never played darts before. The room is not very bright and you can barely see the bull's eye. You are standing along way from the board, but you have an endless supply of darts. You pick up the darts and you just keep throwing them at the target over there on the other of the room even though you are not a good dart thrower and you're not even well coordinated. If you kept throwing darts over and over again what would you eventually hit?

Wright

Pretty soon you would get a bulls eye.

Tracy

Yes, eventually you would hit a bull's eye. The odds are that as you keep throwing the darts even though you are not that well educated, even if you don't come from a wealthy family or you don't have a Harvard education, if you just keep throwing darts you will get a little better each time you throw. It's known as a "decybernetic self-correction mechanism" in the brain—each time you try something, you get a little bit smarter at it. So over time, if you kept throwing, you must eventually hit a bull's eye. In other words, you must eventually find the right way to do the things you need to do to become a millionaire. That's the secret of success. That's why people come here from a 190 countries with one idea in mind—"If I come here I can try anything I want; I can go anywhere, because there are no limitations.

I have so much freedom; and if I keep doing this, then by God, I will eventually hit a bulls eye." And they do and everybody says, "Boy, you sure where lucky."

Now imagine another scenario: You are thoroughly trained at throwing darts—you have practiced, you have developed skills and expertise in your field, you are constantly upgrading your knowledge, and you practice all the time. Second you are completely prepared, you're thoroughly cold sober, fresh, fit, alert, with high energy. Third, all of the room is very bright around the dartboard. This time how long would it take you to hit the bull's eye? The obvious answer is you will hit a bull's eye far faster than if you had all those negative conditions.

What I am I saying is, you can dramatically increase the speed at which you hit your bull's eye. The first person that I described—drunk, unprepared, in a darkened room, and so on may take twenty or twenty-five years. But if you are thoroughly prepared, constantly upgrading your skills; if you are very clear about your targets; if you have everything you need at hand and your target is clear, your chances of hitting a bull's eye you could hit a bull's eye is five years rather than twenty. That's the difference in success in life.

Wright

In reading your books and watching your presentations on video, one of the common threads seen through your presentations is creativity. I was glad that in the promotional material of *Victory!* you state that you need to apply innovative solutions to overcome obstacles. The word "innovative" grabbed me. I guess you are really concerned with *how* people solve problems rather than just solving problems.

Tracy

Vigorous action means you will cover more ground. What I say to people, especially in business, is the more things you do the more experience you get. The more experience you get the smarter you get. The smarter you get the better results you get the better results you get. The better results you get the less time it takes you to get the same results. And it's such a simple thing. In my books *Create Your Own Future* and *Victory!* you will find there is one characteristic of all successful people—they are action oriented. They move fast, they move quickly, and they don't waste time. They're moving ahead, trying more things, but they are always in motion. The faster you move the more energy you have. The faster you move the more in control you feel and the faster you are the more positive and the more motivated you are. We are talking about a direct relationship between vigorous action and success.

Wright

Well, the military certainly is a team "sport" and you talk about building peak performance teams for maximum results. My question is how do individuals in corporations build peak performance teams in this culture?

Tracy

One of the things we teach is the importance of selecting people carefully. Really successful companies spend an enormous amount of time at the front end on selection they look for people who are really, really good in terms of what they are looking for. They interview very carefully; they interview several people and they interview them several times. They do careful background checks. They are as careful in selecting people as a person might be in getting married. Again, in the military, before a person is promoted they go through a rigorous process. In large corporations, before a person is promoted his or her performance is very, very carefully evaluated to be sure they are the right people to be promoted at that time.

Wright

My favorite point in *Victory!* is when you say, "Amaze your competitors with surprise and speed." I have done that several times in business and it does work like a charm.

Tracy

Yes, it does. Again one of the things we teach over and over again that there is a direct relationship between speed and perceived value. When you do things fast for people they consider you to be better. They consider your products to be better and they consider your service to be better—they actually consider them to be of higher value. Therefore, if you do things really, really fast then you overcome an enormous amount of resistance. People wonder, "Is this a good decision? Is it worth the money? Am I going the right direction?" When you do things fast, you blast that out of their minds.

Wright

You talk about moving quickly to seize opportunities. I have found that to be difficult. When I ask people about opportunities, it's difficult to find out what they think an opportunity is. Many think opportunities are high-risk, although I've never found it that way myself. What do you mean by moving quickly to cease opportunity?

Tracy

There are many cases were a person has an idea and they think that's a good idea. They think they should do something about it. They think, "I am going to do something about that but I really can't do it this week, so I will wait till after the month ends," and so on. By the time they do move on the opportunity it's to late—somebody's already seized it.

One of the military examples I use is the battle of Gettysburg. Now the battle of Gettysburg was considered the high-water mark of the Confederacy after the battle of Gettysburg the Confederacy won additional battles at Chattanooga and other places but they eventually lost the war. The high-water mark of Gettysburg was a little hill at one end of the battlefield called Little Round Top. As the battle began Little Round Top was empty. Colonel Joshua Chamberlain of the Union Army saw that this could be the pivotal point of the battlefield. He went up there and looked at it and he immediately rushed troops to fortify the hill. Meanwhile, the Confederates also saw that Little Round Top could be key to the battle as well, so they too immediately rushed the hill. An enormous battle took place. It was really the essence of the battle of Gettysburg. The victor who took that height controlled the battlefield. Eventually the union troops, who were almost lost, controlled Little Round Top and won the battle. The Civil War was over in about a year and a half, but that was the turning point.

So what would have happened if Chamberlain had said, "Wait until after lunch and then I'll move some men up to Little Round Top"? The Confederate troops would have seized Little Round Top, controlled the battlefield, and would have won the battle of Gettysburg. It was just a matter of moving very, very fast. Forty years later it was determined that there were three days at the battle of Gettysburg that cost the battle for the Confederates. The general in charge of the troops on the Confederate right flank was General James Longstreet. Lee told him to move his army forward as quickly as possible the next day, but to use his own judgment. Longstreet didn't agree with Lee's plan so he kept his troop sitting there most of the next day. It is said that it was Longstreet's failure to move forward on the second day and seize Little Round Top that cost the Confederacy the battle and eventually the war. It was just this failure to move forward and forty years later, when Longstreet appeared at a reunion of Confederate veterans in 1901 or 1904, he was booed. The veterans felt his failure to move forward that fateful day cost them the war. If you read every single account of the battle of Gettysburg, Longstreet's failure to move forward and quickly seize the opportunity is always included.

Wright

In your book you tell your readers to get the ideas and information needed to succeed. Where can individuals get these ideas?

Tracy

Well we are living in an ocean of ideas. It's so easy. The very first thing you do is you pick a subject you want to major in and you go to someone who is good at it. You ask what you should read in this field and you go down to the bookstore and you look at the books. Any book that is published in paperback obviously sold well in hardcover. Read the table of contents. Make sure the writer has experience in the area you in which you want to learn about. Buy the book and read it. People ask, "How can I be sure it is the right book?" You can't be sure; stop trying to be sure.

When I go to the bookstore I buy three or four books and bring them home and read them. I may only find one chapter of a book that's helpful, but that chapter may save me a year of hard work.

The fact is that your life is precious. A book costs twenty of thirty dollars. How much is your life worth? How much do you earn per hour? A person who earns fifty thousand dollars a year earns twenty-five dollars an hour. A person who wants to earn a hundred thousand dollars a year earns fifty dollars an hour. Now, if a book cost you ten or twenty dollars but it can save you a year of hard work, then that's the cheapest thing you have bought in your whole life. And what if you bought fifty books and you paid twenty dollars apiece for them—a thousand dollars worth of books—and out of that you only got one idea that saved you a year of hard work? You've got a fifty times pay-off. So the rule is you cannot prepare too thoroughly.

Wright

In the last several months I have recommended your book, *Get Paid More and Promoted Faster* to more people. I have had a lot of friends in their fifties and sixties who have lost their jobs to layoffs all kinds of transfers of ownership. When I talked with you last, the current economy had a 65 percent jump in layoffs. In the last few months before I talked with you, every one of them reported that the book really did help them. They saw some things a little bit clearer; it was a great book.

How do you turn setbacks and difficulties to your advantage? I know what it means, but what's the process?

Tracy

You look into it you look into every setback and problem and find the seed of an equal or greater advantage or benefit. It's a basic rule. You find that all successful people look into their problems for lessons they can learn and for things they can turn to their advantage. In fact, one of the best attitudes you can possibly have is to say that you know every problem that is sent to you is sent to help you. So your job is just simply look into to it and ask, "What can help me in this situation?" And surprise, surprise! You will find something that can help you. You will find lessons you can learn; you will find something you can do more of, or less of; you can find something that will give you an insight that will set you in a different direction, and so on.

Wright

I am curious. I know you have written a lot in the past and you are a terrific writer. Your cassette programs are wonderful. What do you have planned for the next few years?

Tracy

Aside from speaking and consulting with non-profits, my goal is to produce four books a year on four different subjects, all of which have practical application to help people become more successful.

Wright

Well, I really want to thank you for your time here today on *Mission Possible!* It's always fascinating to hear what you have to say. I know I have been a Brian Tracy fan for many, many years. I really appreciate your being with us today.

Tracy

Thank you. You have a wonderful day and I hope our listeners and readers will go out and get *Focal Point* and/or *Victory!* They are available at any bookstore or at Amazon.com. They are fabulous books, filled with good ideas that will save you years of hard work.

Wright

I have already figured out that those last two books are a better buy with Amazon.com, so you should go to your computer and buy these books as soon as possible.

We have been talking today with Brian Tracy, whose life and career truly makes one of the best rags-to-riches stories. Brian didn't graduate from high school and his first job was washing dishes. He lost job after job—washing cars, pumping gas, stacking lumber, you name it. He was homeless and living in his car. Finally, he got into sales, then sales management. Later, he sold investments, developed real estate, imported and distributed Japanese automobiles, and got a master's degree in business administration. Ultimately, he became the COO of a $265 million dollar development company.

Brian, you are quite a person. Thank you so much for being with us today.

Tracy

You are very welcome, David. You have a great day!

About The Author

One of the world's top success motivational speakers, Brian Tracy is the author of may books and audio tape seminars, including *The Psychology of Achievement, The Luck Factor, Breaking the Success Barrier, Thinking Big* and *Success Is a Journey.*

Brian Tracy
www.BrianTracy.com

Chapter 7

GAIL KASPER, LLC

David Wright (Wright)

An internationally renowned public speaker, Motivational Strategist Gail Kasper has come a long way from the nineteen-year-old who moved to California with no job, car, or place to live. Struggling her way to the top, today, multi-billion dollar companies, top CEOs, associations, Ivy League universities, and professional sports teams have adopted Gail's ideas, leadership techniques, and sales programs to increase performance and achievement the "Gail Kasper" way.

In addition to her inspirational keynote speeches, Gail is a highly sought after trainer who has produced live training programs that have captured record responses from leading organizations across the country. Her programs include Customer Service, Communications, Time Management, Leadership, Public Speaking, and Sales.

An in-demand television personality, Gail has been seen across the country on ABC, Comcast, Fox, WB, and CBS where she co-hosted the Emmy award-winning America's TV JobNetwork. She is the current host of the Philadelphia Visitor's Channel.

Gail's time management and goal setting audio CD program, *Make a Decision to Win,* is a life-changing program that has received such rave reviews as "inspiring," "offers great ideas that listeners feel are doable," and, "offers a practical approach to tackle the root cause of a problem and help people achieve their goals."

In the midst of Gail's tour through the Mid-Atlantic States, I had the opportunity to interview Gail and witness her unique ability to read and motivate people as she explained just what it takes to Make a Decision to Win!

The following are excerpts from Gail Kasper's time management and life strategy audio CD program, *Make a Decision to Win*.

Take us back, Gail, to where it all began. How did you become a motivational strategist?

Kasper

About ten years ago, as a manager in a medical research company, I was responsible for departmental and customer training. With my structure and stick-to-itiveness, I knew that I was a good "manager" but not a very good leader. I focused more on the task than on the people. If I had to rate my leadership skills, they were "poor." What I failed to realize was that it was "the people" not "the task" that produced results. It was "the people" who made things happen.

Because I have always loved to learn, I invested in a few leadership programs. At the time, I don't know if I could even define the word "leadership" let alone portray the qualities of a leader. I was amazed to see how little I knew about managing people. I slowly started to incorporate the techniques I learned and the more I focused on the people, the more I saw them grow. Consequently, their personal growth not only affected the department, but also the entire company. The team doubled performance within a six-month time span. They were empowered. This was such a personally rewarding experience, I fell in love with the idea of helping people achieve. From there, I became an employee of one of the largest training organizations in the country so that I could further develop my craft as a speaker and trainer and then eventually went out on my own. My life is a constant evolution but I can honestly say, "I'm doing what I love to do."

Wright

It seems your life has taken quite a few turns. Is this what we can find in *Make a Decision to Win?*

Kasper

Yes, I have had my share of challenges: an abusive relationship, no self-esteem, and a bankruptcy. I often say it took me thirty years to figure out that I actually had a life that was full of choices, and even today, I am growing. *Make a Decision to Win* teaches how to stop living in helplessness and take charge of your life. We've all had instances where we lose a job unexpectedly, or a relationship, or we feel trapped. Our first instinct is that that there is no place to go. We see it as the end. The reality is that it is the beginning—the beginning of something great. It's not the time to surrender—it's the time to go to war! The *Make a Decision to Win* program will help any individual take control of his or her life, set effective goals, and develop the step-by-step processes to achieve those goals. I am very proud of the way that the program has evolved because people have walked away with simple formulas on how to get to success—a success that brings personal and professional contentment. By the same respect it has helped people tackle the obstacles that get in the way of success, such as procrastination, poor time management, and a negative attitude.

Wright

Gail, what would you say is one of the biggest lessons you have learned in getting to success?

Kasper

Follow your passion with a passion. Don't let anyone stand in the way of your belief in yourself. By believing desperately in what you want and who you are, you become unstoppable. When I finally found my passion to be a speaker, I was in the middle of a bankruptcy, I had no money in the bank, and there was no one to borrow from. I was on my own. I barely survived my first year in business with a gross income of a whopping $17,000. That was all I had to survive and build my business. If I had to drive a distance to see a client, I would sleep in my car. If a client owed me even a few hundred dollars, I found myself on the telephone trying to hurry the money along. It was a desperate way to live, but I had a dream. Eventually the hard work and sacrifice paid off and today, I am ranked in the top 15 percent of the most successful speakers in the country. Your passion will drive you. It will not come easy, but it will come.

Wright

Those are good words. Finding your passion in life is so important. Let's get into the details of the *Make a Decision to Win* program. I'm sure our readers want to know specifics. What are the biggest factors that prevent us from achieving our goals?

Kasper

There are two factors: (1) We don't believe the goal is possible and, (2) We don't make good choices to attain the goal.

When we don't believe something is possible, we don't put 100 percent effort into attaining it. If we limit our way of thinking, we will most certainly limit our results. We must believe something is possible.

The other factor is how we execute "our choices," which, if done haphazardly, will also prevent us from attaining our goals. If the goal is to lose weight and you spend your dinners with a giant bowl of ice cream, you're not going to see the results you want. You need to eat balanced meals and exercise. If you want to find a job, it's not going to happen from your couch while you're watching television. You must get out and network, research possible job opportunities, visit with headhunters, and do the things that will produce the results you are seeking.

Wright

Isn't this the obvious?

Kasper

Maybe, but the reality is 90 percent of individuals aren't taking their futures and their lives seriously. I conducted a survey which showed that only 10 percent have a game plan to achieve their goals. We seem to have a difficult time getting our lives on track.

Wright

So what can we do to get on track?

Kasper

First of all, awareness is key. When you are aware of your habits—good or bad—you can ask yourself, is this activity going to get me where I want to go? Will it produce the results I'm seeking? Whether the answer is yes or no, at least you are in a position to make a conscious choice. You are living in reality.

Wright

What exactly do you mean by "living in reality"?

Kasper

Let's just say, it will be very difficult to reach your goals any time soon if you don't live in reality. If we admit that we made a mistake, got off track with the diet, wasted the day and got nothing done, haphazardly spend money without saving, and we recognized our faults, we can change them. When we recognize them, we build awareness, take ownership of them, and are only then capable to make a different choice.

Wright

Is this what you're talking about when you refer to "ordinary" versus "extraordinary" results?

Kasper

Yes. The difference between "ordinary" and "extraordinary" results is having a Strategy—having a game plan every day. We're quick to want the beautiful home and brand new car, but just as "Rome wasn't built in a day," neither is a dream. It's a constant process of being meticulous with your work and personal habits. It's sacrifice and discipline. Creating or following a strategy isn't easy.

Wright

What's the best way to create our strategy?

Kasper

The first thing to do is recognize that we live in a world of strategies. Everything you do has a strategy. When you do wash, there is a strategy—you separate the darks and the whites. When you paint a room, there is a strategy. As a matter of fact, if you have no strategy, the room will be a mess. These facts hold true with our lives. If we have no strategy, our lives become a mess. Would you want to go in the courtroom with a lawyer who has no strategy? Would you want to be operated on by a surgeon who has never performed the operation before? The same thing goes for sports teams. When coaches are on the sidelines, they're not looking at a menu to decide what they are going to have for lunch—they are strategizing. If they don't have a strategy, they lose. Everything in life has a strategy. Isn't it critical to have a strategy for the most important thing—our lives?

Wright

Where do we start?

Kasper

Let's get down to the basics and the foundation. Do you have a daily planning system? If you don't, you need to get one and use it properly.

Wright

What do you mean "properly"?

Kasper

Many who have a daily planning system tend to use it reactively for day-to-day activities. We get a telephone call to schedule a meeting and we open up our electronic organizer or daily planner and insert that activity. To develop a strategy that is going to produce the results you want, you must be proactive and focus on your goals. This means we need to incorporate *our goals* into our daily planning system.

Wright

This is a big process. Where do you start?

Kasper

Once you have invested in a daily planning system, create a Power Plan. A Power Plan is a list of goals that you want to accomplish in your life, short and long term. It's on one list and should include your personal goals such as health, professional development, social, relationship, financial, as well as professional goals like career and education.

Once you have the list in place, isolate the three goals that, once accomplished, would produce the greatest positive results in your life. It's too overwhelming to focus on everything, so focus on the goals that would produce the greatest results.

With these three goals, identify the tasks that need to be done for each goal. So if you have a goal to lose weight your tasks might be: (1) to enroll at a gym, (2) to track your workout schedule, (3) to go to the grocery store to pick up healthy food and, 4) to plan meals.

Once the tasks are listed, place those tasks under specific dates and times in your daily planning system. If you are going to work out at the gym, and plan to go three times a week, indicate those specific dates and times when you will go. Your daily planning system should incorporate everything.

Wright

How often do you review your daily planning system?

Kasper

It should be reviewed weekly to incorporate weekly activities and then daily to update and make changes. What's important is to establish consistency. The more consistent we are with our daily and weekly reviews, the more we will make our daily planning system a part of our lives.

Wright

This is good information but if it's okay with you, since I'm sure our readers can find more detail on your audio CD program, I want to make sure we have time to cover a few more topics.

One of the things I love about *Make a Decision to Win* is your formula for beating procrastination. Your step-by-step formula makes it so easy to follow.

Kasper

Thank you. It's called P-E-R-S-I-S-T—an acronym with each letter guiding you through the process. I have asked audience after audience, "What's the benefit of procrastinating?" Each audience comes up with the same responses: "I can put off a task or maybe someone will do it for me; but there really aren't any benefits to procrastinating." We don't build self-worth or discipline or increase the level of personal contentment in our lives. In fact, procrastinating takes away from who we are and increases our stress level.

Wright

So let's stop procrastinating and get down to the formula.

Kasper

Okay. The P is to make the task a "priority." If we don't make something important, we're not going to make a point to do it. Whether it's saving for the future, going to the doctor's, working out, or getting organized. We have to make "the priority" important which means open up your planning system and write it down. Sit there and look at if you have to, but ask yourself this question: how will it benefit my life to accomplish this task? Just by answering that question, you are making it important.

Wright

What about the E?

Kasper

The E means to "enroll." With "no discipline" being the number one reason people procrastinate, it is important to have a support person who can charge you up to get you started or to ask you how it's going. It should be someone whom you respect and who will be honest with you. This person can get you started and hold you accountable. If you don't have the discipline, just admit it, accept it, and do something about it. Enroll someone who can get you on track and keep you on track.

Wright

What about the R?

Kasper

Record—record, record, record. Record your action steps. What are all the tasks you need to do—the action steps. This will not only make way for a successful outcome but will also give you that productive feeling of working toward the goal.

Now, record how you will feel if you do the task and how you will feel if you don't do the task. Take a piece of paper and draw a line down the middle. If you complete the task, will you feel productive, accomplished, organized, maybe thinner if it's working out, or more stable if you are saving for the future, or more organized if you have kept up on your cleaning? Next, record how will you feel if you don't do the task—stressed, unproductive, depressed? This information can be quite an eye opener.

Finally record your reward. For everything you procrastinate doing you must have a reward if you complete it. You've put it off and put it off, and now you did it. How are you going to reward yourself? Maybe with a new shirt or shoes. Set time aside to read or enjoy a hobby. What is your reward?

Wright

And the S?

Kasper

The S is for schedule. Schedule your first action step and schedule the "drop dead" date—when you want the task to be completed. For the first action step, you must pull out your planner or electronic organizer and schedule the specific date and time you will start the task and work diligently for sixty to ninety minutes—no interruptions. During this time, you will only perform the task that you need to complete.

Now let's look at scheduling the drop-dead date. If you are planning a vacation, that would be the date you plan to go; if it's completing your taxes, that would be the date you are ready to mail them; if it's spring cleaning, when will you finish; if it's to quit smoking, what's the date you will stop?

Wright

The I?

Kasper

The I is for immediacy. As soon as you complete the first action step, check it off. It will give you a feeling of accomplishment. Then schedule the next action step that needs to be done. Again, set a specific date and time to do the task.

Wright

I understand the S is for "Stay the Course."

Kasper

That's right. You may get off track—you are human. Household issues come up, work issues or emergencies. Surrender to them, put it into perspective, pull out your planner, schedule your next action step, and get back on track. You can do it!!

Wright

Last but not least, the T?

Kasper

The T is for "Track your Progress." This is not only the reward you are due when you have completed the task, but it is how you are progressing through the task. We often focus on what we haven't completed and it slows us down. We look at how much more needs to be done—it is overwhelming. Focus on what you have done, look at your progress, continue to schedule the time to work on the task, and you will be amazed at how quickly you pick up the pace and accomplish your goal.

To beat procrastination, PERSIST. If you PERSIST, you will beat procrastination and produce incredible results in your life that will keep you positive and energized to tackle your goals.

Wright

That's one of the things I love about your work, Gail. You break things down into step-by-step "easy" processes that make me feel I can do it. I know you also have a formula to help maintain a "positive attitude." Let me understand this: if I follow the formula, I'll feel better about myself?

Kasper

I'd bet on it. We've talked about the importance of having a strategy in life and our attitude is no different. We need a strategy. We can certainly tell if we are dragging. Even the most up-beat individual has down time. Even the most can-do attitude needs a pump up.

Wright

But it's normal for people to go through down time, particularly during challenging times in our lives. People have breakups, lose jobs, and experience financial struggles.

Kasper

Of course they do and it's normal to experience feelings of loss. But you can either allow yourself to be affected long-term or short-term. You can choose the amount of time during which you will feel this pain. You can either allow an out-of-control situation to control your life or you can take control of the situation.

Wright

I think the question our readers want to know is "how?"

Kasper

There is a six-step formula to follow. What we all need to remember is that the biggest challenge in getting through a tough time is getting started with the process. If we lose our job, we feel like we don't want to get of bed the next day. We just want to crawl into a ball and stay under the covers. Our perception is that this type of response will make us feel better when actually, the opposite is true—it just prolongs the pain. Activity produces results. We must create positive energy. We must get back to our goals.

Wright

So what's the first step?

Kasper

Get your daily planning system. If you do nothing else, crawl out of bed and get your daily planning system or at the very least some paper and a pencil. Again, remember, action produces results. We get so wrapped up in the emotion that it becomes overwhelming. What you're doing here is getting back to logic. You're taking action in a positive way that will not allow you to drown in the emotion. Not a very complicated step, is it?

Wright

No, it seems pretty simple. What's next?

Kasper

Step two is to write down all of your strengths. Regardless of the situation, you are a terrific person who is on this earth for a reason. You're smart and you have talents. Write them down. When you do this, you are making a conscious choice to be positive and empower yourself.

Step three is to make a list of all the things you must do *during that day* to make the day a success. The list might include getting out of bed, taking a shower, going to the gym, or working out at home. If you are looking for employment, it might include picking up the want ads, or if someone just broke up with you, getting dressed and taking yourself to lunch.

Wright

I can handle that.

Kasper

Good. Step four is to pick the three things that if you accomplished them would produce the greatest positive results in your day. Star those things. They are your goals for the day. If you do nothing else, you will want to accomplish these three things.

Step five: Look at your entire list and pick the easiest thing on that list. It does not have to be in your top three. You are going to start with the easiest thing. If you remember the movie "What about Bob?" with Bill Murray, he referred to "Baby Steps." This baby step allows you to get started and once you get started, you are likely to keep moving.

And step six is don't isolate yourself! Call your closest family members and friends and clue them in on what has been going on with you. Our tendency, in difficult situations, is to isolate ourselves and the last thing we need to do is to be alone with our thoughts. Do the opposite. Gain support. People are very understanding of personal challenges. Their words will be an inspiration for your next steps.

Activity produces results and action creates action. You will be on your way to a positive attitude.

Wright

Gail, this is good stuff. And we are running out of time; but tell us, what are some of the other things your program will offer?

Kasper

The *Make a Decision to Win* program is a full-circle program to give you the tools you need to take charge of your life and accomplish your goals. Not only will you focus on developing a vision, but you will also learn how to build on your strengths, create a value system that is synonymous with your goals, create specific personal goals in every aspect of your life, develop your assertiveness skills, and learn how to build your life through progressive delegation and listening skills.

Wright

It sounds like a great program.

Kasper

Thank you. I have been very happy with the response I've had to it.

Wright

Gail, thank you for your time. You've inspired us. Where can we find the *Make a Decision to Win* audio CD program?

Kasper

They are available on Amazon.com or on my Web site, www.gailkasper.com.

Wright

Thank you again. We've been talking to Motivational Strategist Gail Kasper.

About The Author

GAIL KASPER is an internationally renowned high-energy public speaker whose mission is to inspire individual achievement. Gail's unique ability to motivate and read people allows her to personalize her talks, focus on an individual's vision, and establish a simple process to attain that vision.

Multi-billion dollar companies, top CEOs, associations, Ivy League universities, and professional sports teams have adopted Gail's ideas, leadership techniques and sales programs to increase performance and achievement the "Gail Kasper" way.

In addition to her inspirational keynote speeches, Gail has authored the time management and life strategy audio CD program *Make a Decision to Win* as well as the soon to be released book, *Another Day Without a Cage*. As a highly sought after trainer, Gail has produced live training programs that have captured record responses from leading organizations across the country. Her portfolio of programs includes Customer Service, Communications, Time Management, Leadership, Public Speaking, and Sales.

Gail has been seen across the country on ABC, Comcast, Fox, WB, and CBS where she co-hosted the Emmy award-winning America's TV *JobNetwork*. She is the current host of the Philadelphia Visitor's Channel.

Gail Kasper, LLC
PO Box 3610
Cherry Hill, NJ 08034
Phone: 856.354.2145
www.gailkasper.com

Chapter 8

TOM BAY, PH.D.

David E. Wright (Wright)

Today we're talking with Tom Bay, Ph.D., an internationally known speaker and author. He has spent thirty-two years driving home his message that success means making choices and being accountable for those choices. Dr. Bay, who holds a doctorate in media communications, is the author of three books sold internationally, *Rainbows, Whispers, and Shouts: Gifts in Thoughts, Change Your Attitude: Creating Success One Thought at a Time,* and *Look Within or Do Without: 13 Qualities Winners All Share.* He is currently at work on his forth book focusing on leadership.

Tom also does corporate training seminars, workshops, and talks for the general public. His captivating talks reap lasting results. He has inspired thousands of individuals to redirect their energies inward leading to a more productive, positive, and value-based life. He walks his talk—he has served his community and those about him; he has been elected to fifty-two boards of directors and asked to chair forty-eight of those boards.

Tom Bay, welcome to *Mission Possible!*

Bay

Absolutely my pleasure David, thank you.

Wright

So you've written three books and all three have focused on attitude. Would you tell our readers, is it really valid to say attitude is
everything? That's a really strong statement.

Bay

It is a very strong statement David and yes, I do believe that our
attitudes affect everything we do—our careers, our spirituality, our
health, and our relationships in particular. There are different days
and different times that it has more impact but it affects us every
single day. I feel very strongly about that.

Wright

So are there signs that would indicate whether we have a right or
wrong attitude and if so, what are some of these signs?

Bay

In the research I did for the book, David, I talked with thousands
of people over a period of about twenty years. I paid attention to those
around me and those in particular who had a great attitude—what I
later termed a "Right Attitude." I started paying attention to their
mannerisms and their behaviors. The book is really a synopsis of my
notes and observations. Two signs that I recognized in people with
the right attitude are *responsibility* and *ownership*. They take responsibility for their lives and take ownership to make changes to be a
better person.

I think another part of this is that they're dealing with reality and
that's a tough one for a lot of us. When I say "reality," I mean that
things turn bad—you have that stroke of bad luck or you have something that just messes up your day completely but you deal with it.
You say, "Okay, this did happen, now what am I going to do about it?"
As opposed to the attitude of thinking this happened to me and then I
start giving all the reasons why the situation has messed my life up,
or why it screwed up my plans. It doesn't matter *why*—I can't change
why. What am I going to *do* about it? I'm responsible—I have to deal
with the issues that have messed me up! That's where I have control.
I have to be honest, get it out of my system, and then get on with
what I am going to do about it.

People with the right attitude are involved with what they're doing in their life. They genuinely like living and want to have a positive impact on not only themselves but also on those around them.

I find that people with the right attitude consistently have goals. What surprised me is that the goal could be as simple as getting from one end of the day to the other and accomplishing maybe three things I that day. Perhaps they have some little goal they can look back to and say, "Hey, I did this today. I know I set myself some goals and I accomplished them."

Another sign of a right attitude is a sense of humor—being able to laugh things off on occasion. Take a deep breath and realize we're all human—we make mistakes—and maybe make a joke out of some of the things that have happened. In addition to this fact, consider this: will yelling, crying, and screaming change anything? No!

A final sign of having the right attitude is truth and trust—being truthful to others as well as oneself. Be honest—know who you are, recognize your strengths and weaknesses. Work on your weakness and play your strengths. Before you can trust others I must trust yourself.

Wright

You're often quoted as saying, "A single word is the true focus on one's attitude." What is the single word and would you explain that to us?

Bay

This seems so simple. The single word is ONE. It really boils down to the word ONE and in this context, David, *I'm* the ONE. I'm the ONE with the attitude. I'm the ONE to make the choices. I'm the ONE to take action. I'm the ONE to accept responsibility. I'm the ONE to be accountable for my actions. I'm the ONE who has the attitude. It always comes back to the ONE individual.

Wright

Your second book is titled *Change Your Attitude*, subtitled, *Creating Success One Thought at a Time*. That sounds pretty easy, but is it really that simple?

Bay

Exactly, David, it sounds so simple. What really happens is the statement itself is simple but I admit that there are times when it's much more difficult than just the statement itself of "Creating Success One Thought at a Time," especially when I'm dealing with the honesty factor and knowing that I'm the one who has to make these decisions and I'm the one who, after making the decisions, has to take action. And, in many cases, whether it's for myself or others, there are times it's more difficult than just making the statement, "Okay, change your attitude," now I'm going to create success one thought at a time. Yeah, Right! *Sounds* good! But *now* what's going to happen? Nothing—*unless* I take responsibility to change the things *that I control.* David, notice I said *"the things I control,"* that's the critical point.

Wright

I had a good friend, who's also very wise, tell me back in the early '70s that to all of my problems, I'm the only answer.

Bay

Isn't that the truth! Now, see how simple that statement is? It is such a valuable statement, but it's simple.

Wright

You say a major factor of any attitude, right or wrong, is focus. So why is focus so important?

Bay

I think focus is critical. What you're focusing on is going to have the final impact. In other words, you can focus on being healthy or focus on illness; you can focus on forgiveness or revenge. You can focus on self or focus on those around you. You can focus on the problem or focus on the opportunity that the problem has presented to you. That's focus. You or I can go down the line with almost everything we do on a daily basis. We can ask ourselves, "What am I going to focus on today and what am I going to accomplish today?" or, "Am I going to focus on what happened yesterday and why I'm still upset about it, as this day disappears? Am I focusing on building something up or am I focused on tearing something down?" I like to be around people who consistently focus on the positive side.

One of my favorite authors is Iyanla VanZant; she writes about meditation. One of my favorite quote states, "When I exercise I will breathe in health and exhale illness." What a perfect example of focus! Her focus is on the health side and getting rid of the illness—breathing in positive and exhaling negative. Boy, what a great way to multi-task!

Wright

Do you think it's possible to change someone else's focus and in turn, their attitude?

Bay

That question has been asked of me a lot in different seminars and speaking engagements. I really believe you can't change another person. I don't believe you can change their focus or any part of them. What I do believe is you can have an impact and that impact, or course, can be positive or negative. For instance, take yourself, David, you're a very positive person and if I'm around you a lot you will have a positive impact on me. You don't do the changing *I* do the changing.

Often I'm introduced as a motivational speaker and I will correct the introduction in a nice way, but I will point out to my audience I'm not a motivational speaker because really the term is an oxymoron. Motivation comes from within, not from somebody on the outside doing a presentation. If I say something or someone else says something that inspires you to make changes or to do something positive, you take credit for the positive action taken, not the individual who made the statement. So I think using the word inspirational is valid. I don't think we change somebody's focus. We can have a positive or a negative impact in either direction, definitely, but we can't do the changing for someone else; we can inspire others to make changes.

Wright

The focus on your written material has been attitude. Your seminars and keynote speeches always touch on attitude as well. Would it be correct to say that attitude is always your core subject material?

Bay

Absolutely. I have been in the company of many great speakers and wonderful presenters. In the discussions we've had it is the general consensus that "attitude" is the core of who we are. As individuals we are sometimes entitled to have a negative attitude—things seem to be going all wrong. My response to that is express it, acknowledge it, deal with it, and get it out of your system. Then start looking at your choices: What am I going to do about it? It happened to me, it has taken place—now what am I going to do about it?

Wright

You've talked about relationships having a major impact on your attitude. I'd like to explore that a little bit. Would you give our readers a little more in-depth point of view concerning relationships?

Bay

I think having quality is very important. When I'm talking about relationships I'm not necessarily meaning the male-female relationships which is just one facet. The relationships we have with our family, friends, and co-workers and relationships we have with those around us have an impact on everything we do and say.

The critical part of relationship is to have a quality relationship where you can truly be honest. I think people who have consistently good attitudes—right attitudes—are individuals who have a place to be open and honest, and genuine. It takes quality in the relationship to handle honesty. We can't do it all by ourselves, we have to have people around us to bounce ideas and bounce feelings off.

I'm very fortunate, when I have a bad day or I have a bad moment, my better three-quarters—Luann, my wife and friend—allows me to just flat out say it. We have great honesty in our relationship. I've already told her up front, when I get really quiet the reason I'm quiet is because I'm dealing with something internally and I've got to take care of it. It doesn't mean I'm not interested in her, it doesn't mean I'm not in love with her, it doesn't mean I'm angry with her. I'm honest enough to tell her up front that the reason I'm quiet is because I don't want to say something I really don't mean. I definitely don't want to hurt anybody—her or myself. I'm quiet because I really need to take care of something. When I get real quiet she'll recognize it and she'll just say, "I know you need time to yourself," and walk out of my office and close the door. That almost accelerates my being able to deal with my issues and get over it. She is wonderful and I don't take this honesty or our relationship for granted.

Wright

"Ducks and eagles" is an analogy of attitude you use consistently. Will you take a moment to explain to our readers this analogy and the background of your thoughts concerning the subject?

Bay

Dr. Wayne Dyer, a very gifted speaker and author, talks about the "ducks" in life and how they go through each day quacking. This image just stuck with me, David, I couldn't get that image out of my mind. The opposite side of this image is an eagle. Eagles soar—they're very focused. Obviously they're a very majestic bird and they represent our nation as a whole; they're a very grand icon or image.

The contrast between a duck and an eagle is dramatic. In thinking about that we can see they're both birds, they both have wings, but look at the dramatic difference between the two.

One day I was down on Balboa Island, the area where I live, and I was exercising. There tends to be a lot of ducks that hang out in the harbor area. I started thinking about this duck analogy and about what Wayne Dyer said about how some people just quack through life. A woman had come out to feed the ducks, throwing some breadcrumbs. There was just a couple of ducks. Well, the two ducks started quacking right away and as soon as they start quacking they attracted more ducks. Instead of having the few breadcrumbs for themselves, they attracted a whole raft of other ducks and the more they quacked the more ducks showed up. They started stepping on each other and fighting over the bread that was there. It made me laugh and I realized that this is a symbol of our society. Sometimes ducks quack and they attract more ducks.

If you look at this in a business situation for instance, it only takes one duck to attract more ducks. Here's an example of some "quacks": "I don't get paid enough." Quack! Quack! "I wasn't hired for this." Quack! Quack! "My boss—I don't know how she got this job!" Quack! Quack! The quacking attracts more ducks, and they're all adding their own quacks, feeding off each other. When ducks get together and quack, they tend to dirty the place up because they poop. Pretty soon they're all standing around quacking—you hear all this quacking and pooping and realize nothing is getting done. The volume goes up and productivity goes down. Our society really has so many pools of ducks.

Eagles sore—they focus and they soar. What a dramatic contrast between these two birds. They are a really good analogy to our society today. There are so many ducks out there quacking how they can do it better. They wanted to get the job; they got the job and then after a period of maybe two or three months they can tell you everything that's wrong with the company and how they could do it better. Here is where focus comes in again—are you focusing on *solutions* or focusing on *problems*? Ducks focus on problems, eagles focus on solutions. Lift off and soar.

Wright

What is a "belief window"? You use this term often so it must have something to do with attitude.

Bay

Yes, here's the situation: We're all born with a belief window and we look at life through our belief window—from our own personal belief window. We can't get rid of it—it's attached, it hangs out in front of us—we go through life with our belief window. It's crystal clear when we're born.

We also receive a pen to write on the window. Usually our parents are the first to start writing on the window. They write such things as, "You must take a nap, share you toys, be kind to your brother and sister, don't play with your food," and, "Eat your vegetables." When we go through life we process everything by looking through our personal belief window; what's written on the window is what forms our behavior. As we get older we start realizing we've got our own pen and we can wash statements off our window and write our own statements on the window.

As an example, we as parents sometimes struggle when we've written something on our children's belief window and then see our children's behavior different than what we think it should be. It's because they've changed or washed off what we've written on their belief window. They've discovered their own pen and have started realizing, as my son said to me one time, "Hey, Dad that worked for you but it doesn't work for me." In reality he was saying, "Dad, what you wrote on my belief window wasn't working for me; I changed it." So belief windows have a very powerful impact.

Dr. Stephen Covey refers to it as the paradigm shift or changing our paradigm—our viewpoint. I just use the term "belief windows" because I think it's more visual, maybe more understandable. Especially when I'm working with teens I use the belief window as an example of how they can change their behavior by changing what's on their belief window. If things aren't working for them I ask, "What's on your belief window concerning this issue?" It generates some great discussions.

Wright

Would it be correct to say that we must change what's on our belief window to have a change in our attitude?

Bay

Absolutely. I have stated this many, many times over. Your behavior reflects what's on your belief window. The behaviors are always a reflection of what's on a person's belief window. You can say certain things trying to convince people otherwise but your behavior will always reflect your beliefs. Even if it's 180 degrees different from what you're *saying*, your *behavior* reflects what's on your belief window. This is a significant point when you're watching people and they're saying maybe something as dramatic as, "I'm not bias," or, "I'm not prejudicial," but yet their behavior reflects they *are* prejudicial—that's what's on their belief window. The belief window is what designates the behavior.

Wright

Yes. I had the hardest time many, many years ago saying things like "that's not me." Another wise man told me one time a man's actions are a manifestation of his innermost thoughts and it took me forever to figure out that he was absolutely right.

Bay

Isn't it the truth? And you know, that's a great statement! It may be more difficult for a teen to understand that statement but it's the same thing as saying the belief window is what designates your behavior.

Wright

Absolutely. That's what I thought about when you said it. In closing Tom, is there anything you would like to add so our readers might better understand our attitudes toward life and the choices we make?

Bay

Well, to reiterate, and I feel so strongly about this, take responsibility. I'm one who promotes accountability and responsibility. Let me underline it this way: "It's *your* attitude, and it's *your* choice." Don't lose site of that fact. For instance, when I hear statements like, "If it weren't my brother," or, "If it weren't for my teacher," or, "If it weren't for my professors," or, "If it weren't for my boss," etc. Fine, but you're giving your responsibility to somebody else. It's *your* attitude and it's *your* choice. You can be upset with something that's taken place, that's understandable, but what are *you* going to do about it? And that includes changing your attitude—it goes back to ownership.

Wright

Today we have been talking with Tom Bay, Ph.D. He does corporate training seminars, workshops, and talks for the general public. He has inspired thousands of individuals to redirect their energies inward leading to a more productive, positive, and value-based life. And I don't know about you, but I've gained a lot of insight.

Tom, thank you so much for spending so much time with me and answering all these questions on *Mission Possible!*

Bay

Well, thank *you* so much. I am deeply honored and humbled by this opportunity. I know you've done many, many quality interviews David, and this means the world to me, thank you so much.

About The Author

For the past thirty-two years Dr. Tom Bay has been improving the productivity and morale of key executives of some of the most prominent business and organizations in the nation, he has appeared before all the Fortune 500 companies. His consulting company Tom Bay Speaks Up, Inc., located in Southern California, specializing in attitude makeover, as well as presentations on life management, team building, and employee productivity and morale.

Tom Bay, Ph.D.
3027 McNab Avenue
Long Beach, CA 90808
E-mail: TomBay@TomBay.com

Chapter 9

SCOTT McFALL

THE INTERVIEW

David Wright (Wright)

Today we're talking with Scott McFall. Scott founded a five-location chain of human performance clinics. He has inspired success in the lives of over 10,000 private clients. Dr. McFall's methods enhance the performance of companies and individuals. His programs include the use of strategies as diverse as neuro-linguistic communication and self-hypnosis. The methods developed by his firm are used by clinicians internationally. Scott's customized series: "Power Secrets of Sales Magic," "Power Secrets of Management Magic," and "Motivation Magic" are proven, bold platforms for education to corporations and colleges. Scott's techniques and articles have been published in national magazines like: *Sharing Ideas* and *Women's World*. He has been featured in television and radio interviews for over twenty years. Currently, Scott is President of McFall Publishing, Inc. His company is focused on client achievement.

Scott, welcome to *Mission Possible!*

Scott McFall (McFall)

Thanks, it's great to be here David! This is going to be an interesting conversation.

Wright

Well, you certainly have made missions possible for yourself and others. What do you think makes the difference between completion and failure?

McFall

David, for me, it's really a matter of believing in the vision of the project. People who achieve their goals can move their train of thought from the "wishing and dreaming" stages to asking quality questions—the questions that lead to performing the actions needed to get the mission done. When you compare the people who quit with the people who complete their mission in life, it becomes easy to see that the quitters tend to use an internal dialogue. I am describing people who are talking to themselves in their head. They're doubting themselves and debating. In contrast, completers tend to picture the end result, the outcome. They literally "see it," then they use their internal dialogue (the way they talk to themselves) to encourage action. What we can learn from this, really, is the true meaning of the word "vision." Can you see what you want in life? Can you break the project down into the steps it will take to get the thing done? Can you live in faith and security? When you do, you know it is worth taking action immediately.

You might remember the book *The Little Train that Could*. It's a classic used to encourage children. Everyone agrees it's a cute story. The problem is that the plot is not an accurate example of how achievers really think. In the story, the train is saying to itself repeatedly, "I think I can." In real life, if the little train was using a valid success strategy, the story would begin with the little train picturing itself on top of the hill, believing in that picture, and then imagining the internal movie of the wheels rolling up the hill with whatever effort it takes to get there. In that scenario the mind knows it's worth taking the actions to get there. You will do it simply because you believe in the reality of your own vision. We tend to picture our way to success. Vision is used as opposed to talking in our heads.

As we watch the people who fail to achieve, they're constantly taking their emotional temperature instead of focusing on the mission or the goal and the actions it will take to get there. The struggling person is continually in touch with how they're reacting at the moment. It's as if worrying about "making a mistake" has them checking their current reactions constantly. When a bodybuilder's working out, he or she is not in touch with the pain of the moment. Instead, the athlete is focused on the outcome. This outcome focus literally changes the meaning of the current effort from pain to success and pleasure. You are able to get through anything if you remember why it's worth it in the end. You need a secure vision. Once the vision is in place, you can keep the momentum going—simply control the emotions you associate with success. Only allow positive feelings to be connected with the goal.

Wright

One of your specialties is verbal communication, so how does this skill influence completion of missions in life?

McFall

Success begins its flight on the launch pad of visual goal models and is fueled on its flight by excellent communication. Let's pretend you are working on a project as a staff member. You are to follow the leadership of your managers or trainers. If you don't understand the mission, how can you possibly know what to do? If you're leading as a manager and you can't get the plan from your head to the mind of your team, how can they know what to do? You must be able to give structure to the steps needed to get the outcome desired.

Once you have completed your own responsibilities and workload, communicating what you need others to do or think is the single most important skill required to achieve. Do you have a shared view, a common philosophy? You must be able to share information while feeling safe. This truth remains constant in any profession. It's profoundly important in couples and parenting. Even when placing a catalogue order you must be able to get the right information across. Many of us have had the experience of getting the wrong part for a home appliance through the mail, etc. Getting others to understand you and learning to properly understand them is really the ultimate life skill.

When I step into a training environment with a company, the first thing I need to do is let them teach me what they want to accomplish. What problems do they really have? What do they want to eliminate? What's happening right now? If it were going great, if it were going perfectly, what would be different? If I don't listen and understand them, my plan for the improvement of their project would be irrelevant. The feedback given can only be relevant if it stays in line with their specific problems or goals.

Taking in what others are saying while getting around your own assumptions starts the adventure of real communication. You are then able to truly take the time to ask questions that allow you to understand the real message from the other person. The habit of listening with curiosity is the best way to keep your own agenda out of the way. You need to keep your assumptions out of the conversation long enough to connect with what another person is sharing.

I ask myself to become curious while meeting the managers and staff to whom I will speak. At that point, as I tailor the learning ordeals or training to that particular group, it will be on target with the real circumstances they're experiencing now.

It's tragic how often anyone who manages and leads people is on a great mission. They have a sincere team and still end up spending hours or days discussing irrelevant aspects of the situation. Perhaps Jim is talking about how the sales team has issues calling enough prospects. In the same conversation, Alan is talking about the color of ink for a brochure. How about when one party is focused on work while another won't switch gears from talking about their golf game? Neither party is really listening. If we go back to keeping the vision of the shared outcome in mind, it helps the entire group to stay on task.

Some questions to determine whether or not communication matches in a useful way are: Is one person talking about large global chunks of information while another person is only talking about the details? Are we working toward agreement and understanding or are we only noticing the distinctions?

Wright

In your work you talk about "accidental self-sabotage" and how to avoid it. So what can our readers do to eliminate the pain of self-sabotage?

McFall

It's amazing. Everyone self-sabotages to one degree or another. In human behavior, the term "secondary benefit" is used to describe the accidental benefits an individual gets from having a problem. One of the assumptions of the discipline of neuro-linguistics is, "All human behavior begins from a positive intention." If this is true, you might ask, what is positive about self-sabotage? Maybe it gets us out of having to put forth exertion. It can seem that the negative belief limits our risk of experiencing disappointment. As an example, many overweight people choose not to become fit because they begin with the negative belief that they were born that way.

Basically, self-sabotage begins with a feeling of self-pity. We can all relate to Ralphie in the movie, *A Christmas Story*. You may recall when Ralphie is caught swearing, his mother washes his mouth out with soap. Later that night Ralphie is in bed fantasizing about going blind because of soap poisoning caused by his punishment. The point of the fantasy is the sympathy and self-pity caused by imaginary tragedy. This dynamic of wanting sympathy and the structure of self-pity itself is the red flag that an individual is getting into self-sabotage while in pursuit of his or her life goals. If the self-pity dynamic occurs, simply take action—any action—toward the goal and the negative emotion will vanish. With weight loss clients, it's sometimes as simple as getting them to move and grab a glass of water. Like a singer or actor who is nervous before a performance, five minutes into the show the entertainer is feeling calm and doing a great job. If we simply act instead of analyze, self-sabotage doesn't have time to occur.

There is one other side of self-sabotage—debating yourself. Remember, there's only one of you in your head. All action can only happen if you make a decision. When a decision has authentically been made, it is one sided.

People often experience fear while attempting to commit. They think the commitment itself is a trap. The internal dialogue goes something like, "If I decide what I want, then I can't change my mind later." It's okay to know that you are a visitor along each path you take. When you get more information you have the ability to change your goals or adjust the plan.

People need to understand that any disappointment is just a learning experience. The belief that life is a series of learning experiences frees the mind to assess the situation. Either change the plan or implement new actions. You can't learn to ice skate if you aren't willing to fall down. Ask any Olympic skater how much time they have spent with a sore and wet backside. If you want to be great, you have to be willing to start the process with the skills you currently posses.

Wright

How do you plan so that you finish your goals or objectives?

McFall

A ten-step structure can help, David. Step one is actually being able to imagine or fantasize through the completed outcome. This includes what you will see when you reach the goal. You should also know what you will feel when you get it done and how you will talk to yourself internally. At the very least, this step allows you to know how to tell when you have arrived at an objective.

1. Trace the process of getting to the goal from back to front. Go from completion backward and list the steps in order. Once you have done this you possess a step-by-step roadmap for your achievement.
2. List the plan from beginning to end.
3. List all of the resources needed to get that job done.
4. Separate the resources you already have from the ones you need to get.
5. Plan the method to acquire any resources you don't have.
6. List all the daily actions to be taken to acquire the goal.
7. Take action on the plan. Do whatever you can do now. Don't get hung up on the procedure. Keep the plan and the outcome handy so you can review it each day. This allows you to check objectives off your list when you get them done.
8. Review your progress. Notice the activities that are effective. Observe the parts of the plan that are not meeting your expectations.
9. As new information comes in, alter the plan if needed. As you know more you may need to change the process or adjust the goal.
10. Reward yourself for getting it done. You must have an exciting reason to get things done. Emotional rewards are the best. Intellectual reasons to get things done can be true, however, they are not very motivating compared to fun or exciting reasons to participate. Powerful emotions are always more effective than attempting to use intellectual motivation. This is even true for intellectuals.

Wright

Will you share the gift of how you teach clients to deal with obstacles and negative thinking?

McFall

I sure will—that's one of my favorite topics. I love the expression: "it's a big deal." When people are talking about obstacles and negative thinking you have probably heard, " It's a really big deal." People tend to magnify the situation—they make the issue bigger than it is. This makes the situation seem hard to manage. So, the first order of business is to shrink down the obstacles so they're smaller than the payoff.

Many years ago I was the opening act for the late Johnny Cash. Many entertainers were working a huge event called the Norskhostfest. A beauty queen was backstage with us. One of my technical crew members found this woman irresistible and began a conversation with her. My young employee was very sure of himself. He proceeded to crack jokes, tell stories, and compliment the young woman. She smiled at him, laughed, nodded, and seemed to be having a great time.

After about ten minutes of this, her chaperone stepped into the conversation and said, "My boy, you do know she doesn't speak any English at all, don't you?"

At this, the young man said, "Would you tell her that I think she's fantastic?"

The chaperone translated. After the young woman heard the comments in her native language my employee got a huge hug and a kiss. A less confident person would have been embarrassed by the fact that he'd been talking to himself for ten minutes. Our guy was having a great time because the payoff of getting the girl's attention was so much greater than the obstacle of embarrassment. It was fun to see how his confidence paid off.

The basic point is that you will be able to work through any obstacle if the resources you possess look larger in scope or more powerful than the size of the issue you are about to overcome.

Having to purchase a new screwdriver to finish a home improvement project is no big deal to a person with cash. It may seem like the project is impossible to a person who is broke.

See yourself as having the position of strength. Sense that you possess the judgment to perceive the resources you have at your disposal. Know that with persistence you will acquire the ones you need.

Personally, I use this metaphor of swimming halfway across the river. Deciding "it's too far" or "it's too hard" and swimming back would be a huge waste of time. You may find that finishing any project becomes easier when you consider that you are already halfway there. If you just take the time to get started, you can think of it as if you are already halfway to the finish.

Wright

Some people have difficulty knowing which goals and dreams to pursue. How did you find your life mission?

McFall

The direct advice on discovering your mission that comes to mind is, "You get from your career the exact reward that you offer to other people."

Once you know how to add value to the lives of others through your specific talent, skills, or perspective you love your work. If you enjoy it, you will be better at it. When you like what you do, the desire to spend the time growing and learning on that specific topic grows. Actions become easy since you are focused where your sincere interest lies.

Sure, it is true that the career I have enjoyed is primarily the coaching and training of individuals for achievement. My education, coupled with my professional experience, has something to do with my success. In addition to those factors I think that my early formative life had a long-term impact.

I started life born premature. Consequently, I spent the first several months of my life at or around the Mayo Clinic. So, I discovered focus. I was inspired and knew what I was interested in, to some degree, as I came into the world. By the age of twelve I had my first major thoracic surgery—part of my aorta was replaced with Teflon. The major artery was congenitally too narrow for adequate circulation to my lower body. As I spent time in the intensive care unit it seemed to give me some young perspective on mortality. I had to go through a lot of rehabilitation.

Young experiences with pain and waiting, working through physical adversity, and watching my own reactions to self-pity and fear added information about how stress changes the way people sense the world. This type of childhood experience afforded me a birds-eye view of how all those dynamics affected my family, friends, and teachers. Thus began my odyssey of discovery into the world of achievement. The enjoyment of watching my own reactions to obstacles, coupled with my own reactions to achievement, instilled a bit of passion and fun. This early observation inspired a taste for sharing my insights gained through those experiences. "Use persistence while you see past the problems/obstacles in life," and, "Know your outcome," has become the basic common theme. Sharing this message continues to be a blast.

I get to spend time with people who are delighted to find new information and new skills. What could be better than that?

There is another side to this work. I see people in careers every day that they dislike. You can see the light in their eyes dim over time. Having the self-confidence to know that there is a way to combine your individual talents with a profitable career seems to be the deciding factor. Do you know that you can be responsible and fulfilled at the same time?

Wright

When you're consulting for professionals, what's the most common reason they do not complete projects?

McFall

That's a powerful question. The most common roadblock to success seems to be failure to create an action plan after the goal has been set. The executive decides what he or she wants to get as an outcome, meetings are held and then, somehow, a measurable plan of action doesn't happen. Without a structure to follow, there's no way to know whether or not daily effort directed toward the goal is taking place. Eventually, complacency becomes the attitude. At that point the person is thinking, "Well, the heck with it."

In order to fix complacency, a simple checklist of activities is the order of the day. If you've made a decision to achieve a goal, then you can accept the activities and get on with it. This only becomes effective if you have that checklist—that understanding of which actions are supposed to be happening. Because they're there on the list, the actions seem worth it. John Ciardi said, *"Intelligence recognizes what has happened; genius recognizes what will happen."* This little distinction is where the rubber meets the road. Can the person really envision what needs to take place and does he or she know how to take action?

Just indulge me on one more point about professionals. Emerson expressed it this way, *"What you are thunders so that I cannot hear what you say to the contrary."* No technique or knowledge makes up for a lack of sincerity and care. So many people are trying to be smart. If you want to complete your mission in life, being genuine, congruent, and a sincere person is magic. If the individual isn't experiencing genuineness, no amount of effort gets the job done. It's a lesson that should be learned early.

Wright

So how can we stay relevant as we move through our mission?

McFall

Well, relevancy is important and often overlooked. If I rerun all the conversations that my staff, family, and colleagues have started with me over the years, I would find thousands of hours of time spent discussing issues that were completely unrelated to what we were supposed to be working on. The cost for irrelevant banter and focus is huge. I find that people are willing to stay in touch with what's really important only when they are personally invested in the outcome. Do they understand how staying on target buys them free time later? Are they able to notice the pain avoided by getting the goal? Shana Alexander said, *"The sad truth is, excellence makes people nervous."* Because nervousness makes people averse to focus, they become tired and exhausted.

The antidote to nervous people around you is sensing when people need success to seem like a smaller ordeal—making it fun instead of nerve-racking—so that it is more enjoyable to stay focused and relevant in terms of a leadership skill. There's a lot of leverage in knowing how to make focus rewarding. Shrink it down so you can see that your success is attainable. The confidence can be more important than the accuracy.

Wright

In your presentations you have a unique take on learning. Can you give us a picture of why you chose your presentation style?

McFall

Part of it, of course, is just for my own enjoyment. But I believe that people learn better when they're having fun. If you hear people talking about an episode of their favorite sitcom, *Seinfeld* for example, as they're standing around the water cooler, you find out that they can recall in great detail everything in the plot of the show in the episode watched the night before; they only saw it once. On the other hand, when you watch people get ready for a test, they seem to get mild performance anxiety even if they're a good student. Being calm and relaxed, and having fun creates easy learning. Pressure creates difficulty with retaining information.

The presentations I do tend to take advantage of this simple learning fact. The presentations take exclusive, powerful content and deliver the information using comedy or illusions as a visual aid. Audience participation and ordeals are employed to make the central points. Then workshop tasks are used to get the audience totally immersed in the process.

I hear a lot of trainers bemoan that their audiences retain very little of the information the students have been taught. Could this be the trainers' fault? Did the trainer give them event to remember? Was the presentation special enough as an experience to create wonder, to create curiosity, joy, and drama?

There's no doubt in my mind that people would prefer to experience power, fun, and drama as they sit through a speech, rather than just take in information. All I do is give them the information while we're all having a blast.

Wright

How can a person control their internal voice to stay on their mission?

McFall

An individual's conscience is built out of the sound (volume, pitch, pace, tone) of the voice of their most strict or critical parent. Sometimes it's as simple as changing that internal voice to be a bit easier on the individual. To stay on your mission you need the right dose of stimulation and pressure. Too little pressure and a person doesn't care, too much pressure and you're in a panic.

What you want is to treat yourself kindly while you're using your own motivational techniques within your head. This attitude will allow you to succeed while still staying balanced. If you find that you've been too hard on yourself in the past, turn down the volume of that internal monologue—be a bit kinder to yourself. If you have experienced anxiety about finishing projects you might try slowing down the pace a little.

If you find it difficult to care, you may want to turn that volume up a bit. Go at the pace that allows you to get things done but does not cause a sense of being overwhelmed. We see this point illustrated clearly when an athlete is so over-stimulated during a game. Their performance suffers. We call this "choking." There is such a thing as too much motivation. You have a personal measure of intensity that works best for you, and you are responsible to control that level to maximize your success.

Wright

Can you suggest a ritual for achievement?

McFall

You know, this is a little trite, but my favorite is to write down any important goals you may have. It is a profound help to get your mission to the forefront of your mind—read that list every morning, make changes if you need to respond to your situation. Read that list every night. As you do this, you train yourself to notice that your activities are on track. You are able to determine whether or not the specific actions you are taking are helpful in the completion of that list or goal. It can be as simple as a person with a goal of buying a new house skipping a $5 latte every day at the coffee house, and using that $1,800 a year toward the purchase of a house for their family. There are hundreds of examples, but you can see that if you govern today's behavior by the overall picture of what you have to accomplish, you will achieve success.

Another powerful ritual for achievement is to control your assumptions about life. Do you assume that you are a terrific person who deserves success? Do you genuinely like yourself? Do you believe you have a life purpose that gives your actions meaning?

Wright

From some of your volunteer and charity work, it is obvious that the next generation is important to you. Is that what you want us to understand?

McFall

With every single reaction that a child gets from parents, teachers, siblings, etc., you're really setting up whether or not they can complete their missions in life or whether they can achieve at all. Does the child believe that his or her actions affect the outcome when at home or does he or she feel powerless? Early experiences can set children up to believe life is a series of situations that they have no control to change. Worse yet, the young person can end up with parents who punish based on the parent's own mood rather than the real actions of the child. Hopelessness is very dangerous to a child. The child ends up believing that successful goals aren't possible. I believe this starts at the very beginning of life itself. Is the child getting more reward in the form of attention and control from a crisis and hassle, or is he or she getting more reward from success and an even temperament? The father of Gestalt approaches to therapy, Fritz Pearls, stated, "Maturity is the ability to deal with frustrated desire alone." Does the routine of life include ordeals in which a child is getting this lesson or does it not?

As life changes faster and faster in this information age, some of the learning of the past is lost. From time to time we need to assess the cost of the lost traditions in our time to learn and grow. I know families with fifteen-year-old kids who have schedules a Fortune 500 executive could not master. There are many maturity skills that are learned only by having to wait. In our instant culture, our future generations need us to preserve our understanding of the learning process. It includes projecting onto children the expectation of respect and patience. Our future professional culture depends on it. Because of the clarity of the issues facing families and adolescents in the modern world, I do tend to support organizations that focus on creating opportunities in those specific areas.

Wright

What a great conversation, I learned a lot today! I think you're serious about this subject.

McFall

I do enjoy it. It's a great honor to visit with you, David. It's a great pleasure to be involved in the *Mission Possible!* project.

Wright

Today we have been talking to Scott McFall. Scott's customized series: *Power Secrets of Sales Magic, Power Secrets of Management Magic, and Motivation Magic,* are proven bold platforms for education to corporations and colleges as well. In addition, his techniques and articles have been published in national magazines. He's been featured in radio and television interviews for over twenty years.

Scott, thank you for taking the time to talk to us about this important subject on *Mission Possible!*

About The Author

SCOTT MCFALL is a speaker and consultant specializing in communications and human performance. Scott holds a doctorate from AIH in Irvine California. He is a certified trainer in Neuro-Linguistic Programming, an advanced form of motivation technology, from both the American Board of Neuro-Linguistics and the NFNLP. He founded a five-location chain of human performance clinics.

Scott has been intimately involved in the administration and delivery of career education in his field.

Founder of a company that has employed a staff of thirty, Scott is familiar with the challenges facing us in this age of policy change and red tape.

This information packed and entertaining presenter has worked with audiences as large as ten thousand participants and intimate groups of elite trainers.

From the stories of his physical challenges during childhood heart surgery to the powerful, cutting edge communication skills Dr. McFall teaches today, you will be taken on the adventure of a lifetime.

Scott currently teaches his "Secrets of Motivation Magic" keynotes and workshops Internationally.

Scott J. McFall
9201 Desert Road
Bismarck, ND 58504
Phone: 701.250.9290
E-mail: scott@hypnosisconnection.com
www.hypnosisconnection.com

Chapter 10

JERRY STEIN

David Wright (Wright)

Today we're talking with Jerry Stein. Jerry is an Executive Performance Coach for CEOs, entrepreneurs, and corporate executives. He speaks regularly focusing on Leadership and Peak Performance strategies. He is a nationally recognized expert on Executive Peer Groups. Jerry is Chairman of the CEO Roundtable for the DeKalb County Chamber of Commerce, and is a featured columnist on Executive Strategies for the *Atlanta Jewish Times*.

Jerry has over twenty-five years coaching experience and holds advanced degrees in counseling psychology, and marketing from the University of Alabama and Georgia State University. He was named "Executive Coach of Talk Radio" by AOL, and presently serves as Chairman of The Executive Roundtable, a CEO strategic think tank and Coaching organization.

Jerry Stein, welcome to *Mission Possible!*

Jerry Stein (Stein)

David, it's good to be here.

Wright

What's your definition of Executive Performance Coaching?

Stein

Executive Performance Coaching involves the development of a personal relationship between the Coach and the client, designed to enhance the performance of the client. This relationship takes place within the context of an ongoing series of conversations as the Coach customizes a coaching program around the needs of the client.

The dialogue is usually inspirational and motivational, enabling greater development of insight and self-awareness while providing a certain degree of structure and accountability. As the client's focus and direction evolve, a primary skill of the Coach is to ask critically astute questions while using his/her perception to make insightful comments.

All Coaching is not the same; the more experienced Coach will have the range and scope to take the relationship and personal performance work to a much deeper and more far ranging level. The most successful coaching clients are those receptive to their continued learning and growth in this coaching process.

In this case, goal setting and achievement are fundamental components of elementary Coaching, but don't come close to the more advanced work I do with experienced executives open to ongoing personal growth, learning, and self-discovery.

The focus of my Coaching is the development of leadership and peak performance programs, and I've found my work to be effective ranging from the CEO and Entrepreneur to the Key Executive, independent professional, and company leadership teams as they focus on growing their business, personal performance, and quality of lifestyle.

It is the CEO who sets the tone for continued personal development in the company; he is the de facto role model for his people. This culture of leadership values can only start at the top.

Every Coach has his/her own style and approach. It's important to choose one based on chemistry, experience, and qualifications. The short-term benefits can be immediate—getting into action—but the long-term benefits are even more powerful—a sense of direction, purpose, and well being.

As the development of trust and confidence builds, the successful Coach applies astute listening skills while asking great questions, using perception as he/she makes key observations with relevant comments.

A good Coach cares about and works to deepen his/her understanding of the client; a great Coach will quickly recognize and identify client patterns while developing coaching strategies to support the client's performance.

A key client benefit—improved decision-making skills—results from increased self-awareness and directly impacts the client's pursuit of his/her goals.

A Coach typically believes in the client's abilities to create and succeed, and it is the client's passion that is key to the direction of the Coaching program.

The Coach engages the client in a supportive, encouraging, and non-judgmental manner; but also provides a key element of accountability.

The client's issues can vary widely during periods of significant growth or crisis, personal or business. As the Coach works to support the client gaining perspective and insight, the coaching relationship is often referred to as a process of self-discovery, and that's exactly what it is!

The single most deciding factor in the success of the client is a receptive attitude. Without it, there is no coaching relationship; but give me an attitude of "willingness to do whatever it takes," and I'll rejoice in your success!

Wright

What's your background—how did you get into Coaching?

Stein

I grew up in a small town, similar to the one in the movie *Hoosiers*, with a high school class of twelve, surrounded by a sea of competition, performance, and championship teams. Those formative years were important in helping form my core self-image which played a major role in overcoming challenges I faced later in life.

I finished a business degree at the University of Alabama and was having a successful career that included banking, marketing, sales, and real estate. Then I had a stroke. Disfigured and paralyzed, I had learn to speak again while going through years of rehabilitation and a struggle to restart my career.

I knew there was something else I could do to make a contribution to others' quality of life, so I went back to graduate school and completed a degree in Counseling Psychology that included several years of field placements.

Now I was ready, it was second nature for me to develop a private practice—it was just a small business start up! I knew about competition and performance, I knew about Coaching and comebacks, I knew about entrepreneurial fundamentals, and I certainly knew about compassion.

It was natural for me to combine these skills as I developed a practice with more and more clients coming from the competitive business world where motivation, leadership, and peak performance are key. This was the beginning of my professional Coaching career over thirty years ago.

Wright

Jerry, will you share with us a few of your success stories?

Stein

There was the case of Bob H., a new CEO with a four-year-old technology company struggling to get into the black. He first came to me as a participant in the Executive Roundtable with the intention of benefiting from his peers, sharing their best practices.

With a few targeted questions, it soon became apparent to me that his board of directors was seriously micromanaging Bob, which was incompatible with the strong leadership needed to make critical decisions and move the company forward. The Board was international in scope with high profile, wealthy bankers, venture capitalists, and strong egos.

The key to Bob's performance was developing his mindset and understanding his role as a CEO. Bob needed to be proactive and make decisions, filling the void of power and taking control. He needed to exercise his leadership on the Board and refuse to be micromanaged and intimidated by their wealth and position.

This was a complicated scenario; it took a year as Bob went through the process of implementing a strategy, reformatting his board, and making key hires within the company. Six months later the company was in the black. I consider an eighteen-month turnaround in this situation a step below a miracle!

Wright

Do you always expect major breakthroughs with your clients?

Stein

(laughing) Well David, it's really the clients' decision, it's their success. The key question is: *How far do they want to go?* Are they going to commit to doing whatever it takes? I'll give them everything I've got. The question is, are they gonna do the same?

Take the case of Bill M., a wonderful and very talented guy, but very shy. Initially, Bill was a real enigma. He would come to the Roundtable but just hang back. He even would physically move his chair just outside the group turn his body at an angle, making little if any eye contact.

Here was a guy who had a $500 million P and L responsibility with a major company and, through a series of circumstances, found himself in transition. Bill had loads of talent, great people skills, a strong strategic background, and an incredible reputation in his industry. There was only one problem—he didn't see himself that way.

During this time, Bill was offered the CEO position of a $125 million company and he couldn't believe it. He didn't understand why this company would offer him the job! I knew it was never going to happen for Bill until he got his mindset right; he had to regain his self-image.

This is a good time to remind you, I work with successful executives and entrepreneurs, and Bill was no exception. Tiger Woods had a couple of tough years in the middle of his career before turning it back around, and that's exactly how I saw Bill. I had to hang in there with Bill and not push—he was already pushing himself, never missing the Roundtable or his individual Coaching sessions.

I helped Bill write a career and lifestyle description, he then went out and developed it, becoming the Executive Director of a major professional association with a lucrative income. This was part of his plan as he raised millions of dollars to establish one of his life-long dreams—the founding of a private school in Charlotte, North Carolina. The school opened last year and has a five star rating!

Wright

Wow, I like that! Your Coaching approach depends on "just how far they want to go!" Do you work only with CEOs?

Stein

No, but I always work with decision-makers. There was Linda K., a key staffer in the public affairs office of a high profile government agency. Her job as the senior speechwriter was to make her boss look good, and although politically connected, he was a poor communicator.

With a dominating and demanding personality, communication was strained; Linda felt intimidated and insecure. After coaching her in various scenarios, she developed a rapport with her boss and was *invited to join his staff in Washington when he became Surgeon General of the United States.*

In this case, Linda needed the confidence to express herself in dialogue over time, making her performance and value to her boss more visible.

It was her choice: act like wallpaper and blend in, or show up in the world. She's a great lady and I'm so proud of her!

Wright

That's very interesting Jerry. Have you worked with strong egos and CEOs at the top of their game?

Stein

Oh yeah. Take the case of Chris P. He was bright, physical, and tough. He had a directional drilling company and was always looking to grow. His goal was to increase annual revenues from ten to fifteen million dollars within five years. I shared my perspective with him, saying that the company's present employee infrastructure, communication skills, and talent base wouldn't support that kind of growth. He didn't get defensive; he went out and changed it. After working with Chris and his leadership team for a year, the company's talent bank, culture, communication, recruitment, and accountability improved. A year later *revenues hit fifteen million dollars, which was four years earlier than planned.*

On the other end of the scale there was the case of Michael P., a junior officer in the U.S. Rangers, who was medically retired after a significant knee injury in an airborne assault jump. He was a good soldier and a great guy. The military was his planned career path, so naturally he was at a loss on how to make the transition into civilian life after his premature retirement.

Within nine months of beginning his coaching program, Michael had established his company delivering leadership training to executives in simulated field exercises, *getting a check for $135,000 from his first client!*

Michael is a dedicated family man with a supportive wife. He has strong values and clearly defined roles in his life. He was a good soldier and maximized his coaching results with structure, discipline, and attention to detail.

Wright

These are great stories Jerry! What common themes have you noticed among the executives and entrepreneurs using an Executive Coach?

Stein

It would seem that successful people are always open to learning and growth; by that definition they are always in some type of transition. So the generic answers are simply they want to take their life and career to the next level and understand growth is fundamental to sustaining their current success.

However, when we look more closely, their situations usually involve significant periods of growth or crisis, either personally or professionally.

Growth and opportunity frequently come out of crisis, but you're not going to have anyone wish for a crisis, so my colleagues rarely use that word unless they specialize in "crisis management." I have done work in this area and enjoy it, but obviously it's very situational. Sometimes a crisis takes time to play out; a Coach frequently can see it coming.

Take the case of Kevin M., a highly regarded attorney with a prestigious law firm. He came to me with a "time management" problem. Just prior to making partner, he had a few years where he didn't quite make his bonus.

His firm had been cutting the billable hours he submitted and the net effect made him ineligible for his bonus. Well, Kevin didn't have a time management problem—he had a severe conflict with the values of the firm, which he was loath to admit.

Kevin eventually understood the bottom line and executed a strategy changing firms with a culture more compatible with his values. It took about a year for this process to develop and come to a head. Kevin had to learn how to externalize his internal conversations and understand what was important to him. He was paying a heavy price for being passive and non-confrontational, a rare trait in his field of endeavor.

Wright

Do you have one last favorite story you would like to share with our readers?

Stein

Oh yeah, I call it *"The Day the Sky Fell in Atlanta."* Bob K. was the true definition of the little engine that could! He was the CEO of an engineering firm and a Georgia Tech graduate. When he came to the Roundtable, his business was dead in the water!

A large commercial billboard fell and killed several people. The insurance companies were not happy and the sign manufacturers were in a panic. The insurance company hired Bob to do a failure analysis of the structure. Bob shrugged his shoulders thinking it was just another routine short-term project, but I hopped on it like a hot potato!

Bob needed to learn how to get more visibility for his business and use the leverage of his strong achievements to position his company. Bob was asked to speak to 150 members of the sign manufacturers association; he didn't want to do it, he wasn't a speaker. We got him prepped and ready—he hit a home run!

Results were offers of a column, a job, and a major project for his firm. In addition, he got a major speech and newspaper article out of it, titled: "The Day the Sky Fell in Atlanta"! I give Bob the credit for his breakthrough. He showed incredible persistence as I pushed him hard; it didn't come easy or quick for him. I hold Bob in the highest regard.

Wright

Jerry, you've received national recognition for your innovative work and contributions in the field of coaching and facilitation of executive peer groups. Will you share a little about the Executive Roundtable and how you came to develop the "Stein Model"?

Stein

The Executive Roundtable is an *experiential peer group* where members *Share Best Practices Impacting Personal Performance and Business Growth.* The group is facilitated by an Executive Coach, trained and licensed by my organization, and is a unique proprietary group model we've developed over the last twenty years.

The *Atlanta Journal* newspaper did a feature article on my work. The national newswires picked it up going from the East to the West Coast. I started getting invitations to speak and Coach across the country, speaking to various professional associations and working with different companies as I developed or delivered coaching programs.

Our group model has a closed and confidential membership structure, designed to have an immediate learning impact transferable to the real world. The Executive Roundtable Corp issues the license to facilitate the use of our Stein Group Model©.

Wright

Why has the Roundtable been so successful?

Stein

I believe it has to do with the unique experiential structure of our model, combined with the skilled facilitation of a well trained professional Coach. The learning modes in our model are comprehensive and include auditory, visual, and kinesthetic elements.

Members bring a range of topics they wish to explore. Once polling members, the Coach and facilitator will choose the most appropriate set of topics relevant to the group. Some topics are addressed over a period of time, but the model incorporates individual and group work, having a powerful impact on the client takeaways and transferable skills.

"Coaching in the round" is rare, not many Coaches have that level of skill development, but it is applied intensively along with other key methods. We integrate coaching in the round into our proprietary model along with shared best practices and proactive group facilitation.

I can describe what love feels like to you or the enjoyment of a wonderful meal, but it doesn't do justice to the experience! Research has demonstrated repeatedly that people remember a small percentage of what they hear, but much of what they feel and what they experience; this especially applies to learning experiences.

I've completed a survey of hundreds of Roundtable members who've participated anywhere from six months to three years, and not one has reported experiencing anything like it in a corporate training or coaching program.

Wright

What's your theory of leadership, performance, and growth? How do you apply this in your Roundtables?

Stein

I believe that a professional's external performance is directly correlated to their personal sense of well being. For every unit increase in a client's personal sense of well being, there will be an exponential increase in their external performance.

Your personal sense of well being is directly related to how authentic you live your life. This authenticity is based on how congruently your internal and external conversations express your values—how you show up in the world.

I facilitate the Executive Roundtable and my individual Coaching sessions around the structure of four questions which are continually reflected upon:

What do you want your life to look like a year from now?

What challenges do you face in making that happen?

What commitments do you need to make to face those challenges?

What price will you pay if you don't make those commitments?

Wright

You are a columnist for the *Atlanta Jewish Times* on Executive Strategies. What themes do you explore and how do you get your stories?

Stein

Thanks for asking David, that's more fun than a barrel of monkeys!

My theme is around leadership development and personal performance—how that plays out in everyday life. I get to have fun reflecting on people's victories and all too human mistakes.

My column is not meant to be a political one, my intention is to entertain, inform and inspire you. But it's difficult to refrain from comment on the leadership and performance of our elected officials, as they give us so many examples to learn from, while we examine our values and ask ourselves what kind of leadership do we want for our country.

We've trusted our national and corporate leaders, and I feel we have been let down. We can't just throw peoples' pensions away, forfeit the trust of lifelong employees and not make that a criminal offense! And what about leadership's responsibility to tell the truth and demonstrate a major degree of authenticity when committing our boys to life and death situations? Strong leadership is about connecting with your people and sharing a vision. Deception should not be a part of that vision, but the focus on accountability should. We the people deserve to have higher expectations of our corporate and government leaders. Truman got it right, "The Buck Stops Here!"

My column involves anything relating to strategies on motivation, leadership, personal performance, and growth, and that leaves the field wide open! So, I do a lot of reflecting and I have fun.

Wright

Jerry, I understand you have been appointed the Chair of the CEO Roundtable for DeKalb Chamber of Commerce in Atlanta. I want to offer my congratulations. I understand there is an interesting twist to this story.

Stein

I submitted a proposal almost two years ago to develop the CEO Roundtable for the Chamber. This proposal got lost but the University of Georgia Small Business Division found it and tried to get it off the ground with no success. I had not been contacted about it or acknowledged for having developed it.

Now fast forward: I was observed making a presentation at the Chamber's Business Expo by the Executive Director, he approached me and asked if I would become the Program Chairman; to organize, develop, and deliver the CEO Roundtable program. He was making my proposal back to me! He is a great guy and we laughed about it when I explained what happened.

The moral of that story is simply: it's easy to borrow someone's ideas; it's another to implement them. You are unique; you are your USP (Unique Selling Proposition). You just have to know how to package and position yourself to your target market. Anyway, that experience gave me a great deal of satisfaction—I'm sure you can relate to that.

Wright

Today we've been talking with Jerry Stein. He's an Executive Performance Coach for CEOs, entrepreneurs, and corporate executives. He has over twenty-five years of Coaching experience and holds advanced degrees in Counseling Psychology and Marketing from the University of Alabama and Georgia State University. As we have found out here today, he knows a whole lot about Leadership Development and Peak Performance Coaching.

Thank you so much, Jerry, for being with us today on *Mission Possible!*

Jerry

It's been a pleasure visiting with you David.

About The Author

Jerry Stein, Executive Performance Coach and Keynote Speaker, has over twenty-five years experience developing Coaching and Performance programs for CEOs, Entrepreneurs, Key Executives and Leadership Teams.

Jerry is CEO of The Executive Roundtable, is a Columnist on Executive Strategies for the Atlanta Jewish Times, and is Program Chair for the DeKalb Chamber Roundtable.

Jerry was named Executive Coach of Talk Radio by AOL and produced the award winning video, Getting Unstuck.

He has advanced degrees in Counseling Psychology and Business from the University of Alabama and Georgia State University.

Jerry is a Certified Master Performance Coach, a fourteen-year member of the National Speakers Association, and a nationally recognized expert on Executive Peer Groups.

Jerry Stein
Phone: 770-988-0500
E-mail: jerry@jerrystein.com
www.CEOperspectives.com

Chapter 11

AVA DIAMOND

David Wright (Wright)

Today we're talking with Ava Diamond. When people are ready to *rock the status quo*, they think of Ava Diamond. As President of the Diamond Success Group, she works with people and organizations to take them from where they are to where they want to go, and helps transform "business as usual" into extraordinary success.

Ava's expertise comes from her experience as an educator, a Fortune 100 computer company manager, a non-profit executive, and a consultant. She distills the lessons she's learned into powerful principles and strategies for transformation and success.

Her latest book, *Great Quotes from Feisty Women,* combines inspiring quotations with Ava's own down-to-earth wisdom. She is also co-author of *Real World Management Strategies that Work.*

Over the last twenty years, thousands of people have benefited from her programs on personal excellence, leading in today's world, success strategies for women, thriving though change, and winning with diversity.

Let's start with a big question—if people want to reach their full potential, where would they start?

Ava Diamond (Diamond)

It's critical to start with three things—knowing *who you are, why you're here, and what you want.*

Who You Are:

The place to begin is having *deep knowledge of yourself*—of who you are at the core of your being. You can begin by taking some quiet time and asking yourself these questions, one at a time. Spend a little bit of time reflecting on each one before you move to the next.

What is most important to you in your life?
What are your most cherished values?
What have been the happiest moments in your life and why?
What do you most enjoy doing?
What fulfills you?
How do you communicate with the innermost parts of your soul?
What part do relationships play in your life?
What brings you joy?
What would you be doing with your life if money were no object?
What gifts can you share with the world?
What would you do if you knew you could not fail?
What do you want to be remembered for?

These questions, when genuinely thought through, begin to get you in touch with who you really are and what matters to you. And remember, there are always two answers to every question—the one that sounds good, and the one that's true. It's important to go deep enough to get to the one that's true for you.

One way to do this is to answer a question, then ask yourself, "Why is that important to me?" Then take that answer, and ask, "Why is *that* important to me?" Then take that answer and ask, "Why is *that* important to me?" Then take that answer and ask, "Why is *that* important to me?" You might be surprised where those answers take you. Use this process for each question.

Why You're Here

From there, you can discover why you are here—*your life purpose.* Your purpose transcends your goals. It's the big picture. It answers the question, "What are you here to do?" It's inspiring, engaging and clear. It creates a passion, a feeling of significance, a focus for your life. Identifying your purpose enables you to choose what to give your time, energy, and attention to rather than being sidetracked by the next bright shiny object.

I'm embarrassed to say that throughout my childhood and early adulthood, I was famous for my "five minute ideas." That's what my friends and my family called them. I'd get a big idea, a big vision, pursue it briefly—then I was off to something else that caught my attention and captured my imagination. My life lacked focus. Once I discovered my life purpose, I found that focus my life had been lacking,

How do you get clear on your life purpose? Here is a five-step process:

First, identify your UDQs, your unique, distinctive qualities, such as intelligence, curiosity, exuberance, integrity, commitment. To identify these, you might think about how you'd describe yourself, or qualities that others have pointed out to you.

Second, think of the impact you'd like to have on the world, and on those you interact with. How will people and the world be better off as a result of your having lived your purpose?

Third, make a list of as many action verbs as you can think of. Try each one on. Circle those that get you excited, that speak to you. Then narrow it down to two or three. Examples of action verbs might be: build, motivate, educate, defend, discover, communicate, share, produce, work, explore, and improve.

Fourth, identify whom you're here to impact or help.

Fifth, combine your work in the first four steps into your Life Purpose Statement. Play with the words. Combine them in different ways. Write down your purpose, go off and leave it for a while, then come back to it. Is it simple? Clear? Easy to understand? Brief enough to remember? Does it inspire and excite you?

As an example, here's mine: *To make a difference by inspiring and empowering people to live their dreams.*

When you have your statement, post it where you will see it. Carry it in your wallet. Engage with it each day. It will provide you with inner guidance, direction, and focus.

What You Want

Once you are clear about who you are and why you're here, it's time to get clear about *what you want*. Many years ago, I was introduced to a wonderful exercise—creating a list of 100 things I want to be, do, and have. I recommend doing this exercise, and letting your imagination soar.

Imagine that there are no limits, that money is not an object, that your past does not dictate your future, that all of your dreams can come true. And then make your list.

In your deepest heart, in the whisperings of your soul, what do you truly want to be, do, and have? Get it on paper—it's the first step to creating those things in your life.

Wright

But for most people, aren't those limits reality? Don't they have economic limitations, and a current set of circumstances in their life?

Diamond

Yes, these things *seem* very real. Yet it's important to realize that you see things not as they are, but as *you* are. You see, you are born with a "blank slate." And over your lifetime, your slate is filled with messages from your parents, your school, your peers, and your faith, by your previous life experiences, by the media, and by every other thing that has had a chance to imprint itself on your thinking. All of this then forms your unique way of viewing the world. It's like a set of lenses or glasses that you see the world through.

How you see and think about something—your perception—creates your experience of it. So, in reality, your thoughts create your life experience. They form a kind of "mental mold" that the Universe then fills. I once heard Ilyana Vanzant, author of *One Day My Soul Just Opened Up*, describe the process. She talked about the creative power of the universe being like cookie dough. Your thoughts are the cookie cutters, going out and plucking shapes or experiences out of this creative stuff of the universe. Your life, then, is created by the thoughts you think and the beliefs you hold.

Except that you tend to forget this. Your reactions appear to be automatically triggered by people and circumstances, and you simply react. You forget that there are still *choices* you are making in every moment, generally unconsciously. Everything in your life today is a result of choices you made in the past—all of it. Your thoughts and beliefs, which result in your choices, are magnets for the experiences that come into your life.

There's a wonderful story that circulated a few years ago about two men who went fishing. One man was an experienced fisherman, the other wasn't. Every time the experienced fisherman caught a big fish, he put it in his ice chest to keep it fresh. Whenever the inexperienced fisherman caught a big fish, he threw it back.

The experienced fisherman watched this go on all day and was becoming exasperated as he watched the man throw back the big fish. "Why do you keep throwing back all the big fish you catch?" he asked.

The inexperienced fisherman replied, "I only have a small frying pan."

Is it true that he could only keep fish that would fit in his pan? Of course not! He could have cut up the fish, used the other guy's pan, or bought a bigger pan. Yet he *perceived* that he could not keep any fish that was too big for his pan. He *perceived* that he could only keep small fish. He *perceived* that his small pan meant small-fish-catching opportunities.

It's important to look at what your thoughts and perceptions are telling you about your opportunities. Are you telling yourself that it's a tough economy, that business is slow, that your dreams are not in your reach? Or are you confident that you can be successful in any economy, that business is great, and that your dreams are within your grasp?

This is critical—this is huge—and this is why so many people's lives are not working! If that thought makes you uncomfortable, realize that you can take responsibility. And what is that? Responsibility is simply the "ability to respond," the ability to *choose* your response. You cannot afford to blame circumstances, conditions, or what other people do or don't do for the conditions in your life. You *always* have choices.

When I discovered this many years ago, I was not happy. This did not sound like good news to me. You see, I didn't get to be a victim any more. I couldn't point to things outside of me and blame them for the conditions in my life. I had to take responsibility and use that ability to respond. I had to begin to align my thoughts and my consciousness with my desires. I had to become conscious, to know that there was a creative power in the universe, and that I could use the power of thought and affirmative prayer to re-create my life. And now I know that this is wonderful news—that my life is an out-picturing of my thoughts.

I attended my thirtieth high school reunion a few years ago and was talking with a group of friends, when a guy I'd only known slightly in high school joined the conversation.

"I think we ought to have our next reunion in five years instead of ten—you know, a thirty-fifth reunion instead of waiting 'till our fortieth," he said.

I asked him why, assuming he'd say something like he was having such a wonderful time, or that it was great to see people he hadn't seen in so long.

"Well," he said, "if we wait ten years, some of us will be dead."

My jaw dropped. I was speechless. Heck, most of us weren't even fifty yet! I thought about his comment all the way home. What a way to think! I wonder what his life and his health are like now, five years later. I wonder what experiences he's attracting into his life with those thoughts. I wonder if he'll be around for our fortieth reunion.

Wright

You've got me wondering, too! Okay, if people want to use the power of thought in their life, where do they begin?

Diamond

I think you have to begin with a willingness to grow. There are things that have to happen on the inside as you move toward your dreams. You need to let go of your self-limiting beliefs. You need to let go of what stands in the way. You need to be willing to move beyond your comfort zone, to stretch beyond your current limits, to grow beyond your current circumstances.

The universal imperative is "grow or die." To be more successful, I'd suggest that you identify a huge goal—a quantum leap. And here's the reason: things in your comfort zone feel pretty attainable. You might have to stretch a little, but most of us are okay with that small, incremental change that's required. But when you go after a quantum leap, you're going to have to grow. You're going to have to change. You're going to have to step boldly out of your comfort zone into what I call your "learning zone."

When you go after this huge goal or dream, it will change your life in three important ways: First, you will listen to the deep desires of your soul and will get in touch with what you *really* want. Second, you will have to break through limiting, self-defeating thoughts to a place where what felt impossible just a short time ago now feels possible—not because the circumstances have changed, but because *you* have changed. And third, who you become as you stretch and grow to accomplish this goal or dream will be as important as the accomplishment itself. You will emerge stronger, more confident, more powerful, and able to overcome obstacles that stand between you and your dreams.

On a very practical level, you can use what I call PowerTools to "See It and Be It." You can use visualization and affirmations to build your faith in your goal. You can think about and believe in your dream every day. You can use your imagination to make it as real as possible, marinating in visual images of how you will live, how you will behave, and how you will feel when you've attained your goal. You can use positive self-talk to reframe your thinking. Using these tools daily builds your success mindset.

Wright

I know you talk a lot about "rocking the status quo." What do you mean by that?

Diamond

I think you have to have a level of dissatisfaction with the way things are—with the status quo—before you are willing to undertake radical change. Otherwise, why bother? You have to be willing to shake things up, to ask deep questions, to be willing to *really* go for it. You have to stop holding yourself back because you're afraid.

You have to commit to take action! A positive attitude is not enough—you have to be willing to *take action* to have greater success. You need motion, you need movement, and you need momentum if you want to have an amazing life.

Rocking the status quo means committing to do something different—to push the boundaries of your experience. How do you do it? You can start with these ten things:

1. *Give up whining and complaining.* You are never moving in a positive direction when you're busy whining or complaining. Stop it. Now.
2. *Set goals.* Having a vague idea of where you want to be won't take you there. Being clear about what you want to achieve, and creating a plan to get there will.
3. *Stop sitting in front of the television.* Watching television occasionally to unwind or to tune in to something educational or entertaining won't kill you, but if you find

yourself mindlessly sitting in front of the tube night after night, staring blankly at the screen, you could definitely be using your time more effectively.

4. *Learn something new.* Read books, listen to tapes and CDs, and talk with people who are wiser than you are or who have more experience in an area you want to know about.
5. *Be yourself.* Don't waste your time or energy trying to fit someone else's idea of who or what you should be.
6. *Believe in yourself and your abilities.* Really.
7. *Define success for yourself.* Not what your parents, partner, or society says—what *you* say.
8. *Don't let the naysayers drag you down.* They don't know what they're talking about. Don't let other people's opinions about you or your success stand between you and your dreams.
9. *Be bold.* Be willing to say what you think, go after what you want, and take risks.
10. *Learn what you can and move on.* Failure isn't fatal. Don't dwell on setbacks. They'll inevitably happen if you're taking risks. Grab the learning, apply it and move forward.

Wright

Once people have this knowledge, what advice would you give them to help them be more successful?

Diamond

I believe that true success lies at the *intersection of talent and passion.*

Let's take *talent* first. We all have things we are naturally good at—things that come easily to us. We feel natural, "in the flow" when we're doing these things. It might be analyzing numbers, working with our hands, nurturing and caring for others, innovating and inventing, selling products, creating music, leading other people, building relationships, working with details, or any number of other things.

Statistics prove that if you are working in an area in which you have natural talent, you are up to 50 percent more productive than someone who is "working uphill" in an area that's not their natural talent.

I was lucky enough to discover my talent early in life. I tell a story in my speeches about the time when I was seven years old. I walked outside one early July afternoon and got an exciting idea: if my dad cleared out some of the stuff in the garage and set up a card table and some chairs, I could have a little school for the other kids in the neighborhood.

I went into the house and told my dad what I wanted to do. "It's summer," my dad said. "Don't you want to have fun instead of focusing on school?"

"It *will* be fun," I insisted, I'm gonna be the teacher!"

My dad got up from watching golf on television and took me out to the garage to set up my school. My mom helped me round up paper, pencils, crayons, and elbow macaroni and string. I also brought out the pink plastic shoe I'd learned to tie my shoes on. Then I went out recruiting. I invited a few younger kids on my block to come to my school the next day. By the next morning, I was leading those kids in drawing, coloring, learning to tie their shoes, and making macaroni necklaces. A career was born.

In the third grade, I volunteered to work with the class of children with Down's Syndrome in my school. By junior high, I knew I wanted to be a teacher. My first career was teaching high school English for four years. As I moved into the corporate world, I began to train and consult, and then I founded a consulting and training firm in 1995.

It all started with a little seven year-old girl who somehow knew what she loved to do and what her innate talent was. When I'm in front of an audience giving a speech or a workshop, I know I'm doing what I was born to do. I feel "in the flow," that I'm at my best, that I'm expressing my innate talents.

Which leads me to the other part of that success intersection— *passion.* When you are living and working with passion, you feel alive and exhilarated. Your energy is high and you have a clear sense that what you're doing is important.

It takes great courage to follow your passion. Mother Theresa was a wonderful example of this. Her passion called her to dedicate her life to helping the poor, the sick, and the dying. What if her parents had said, "Agnes [her given name], why don't you just get a job like everybody else?" What would the world have lost if Mother Theresa had not followed her passion?

James, a man I met a few years ago, helped deepen my learning about passion, and about getting in touch with the meaning of one's work and contribution. A few years ago, my mother spent a couple of days in an emergency room unit. The hospital had a bed shortage and was not able to transfer her to a regular room for two days. As I spent time there, I couldn't help but notice one particular hospital employee.

He came by every few hours to empty the trash and mop the floor. He was an older man with curly hair and a huge smile. He'd hum to himself as he worked. Each time he came by, he'd spend a few minutes flirting with my mom and joking with my sister and me. He was a delightful man who clearly enjoyed what he did.

As I watched him, I couldn't help but wonder, "Why is this guy so happy? His tasks don't look like much fun. All day, he has to empty trashcans and mop the floor. Maybe he even has to clean the bathrooms. I wonder why he's so cheerful." I was really puzzled.

By the second day, I couldn't stand it any longer—I had to ask. "James, your work doesn't look very fun to me. Yet you walk around singing all day. You talk to people and you make them laugh. How do you have so much fun mopping the floor?"

James stopped and thought a second. He leaned on his mop. He looked me directly in the eye and said, "You don't understand . . . my job's about a whole lot more than mopping."

I was all ears. I figured he was going to tell me about some other, more enjoyable duties that I didn't know were part of his day.

"You see, when people come in here, they're all stressed out. Something bad happened to them or to someone they care about. They usually don't know what's going to happen. I get to make a difference. I get to joke with them or say something nice or tell them everything's gonna work out. *I get to be something good that happens to them today.*"

I spent a lot of time in that hospital. I met doctors, nurses, surgeons, and administrators. But I didn't meet anyone who brought as much passion to his or her work as James.

So back to your question, David: what advice would I give someone who wanted to be more successful? Live and work at the intersection of talent and passion. Discover what you're good at, combine it with your passion, and let 'er rip!

Wright

Sometimes when people decide to go after a goal, or to make a change, it seems overwhelming. How do you advise people to get started?

Diamond

That's a great question. I discovered a new approach for myself when I went *from zero to sixty* in five months. I call it the "Chunk-It-Down" approach.

In March of 2001, I decided to do the Avon Breast Cancer walk—sixty miles from Fort Collins to Boulder over three days. At first it seemed like an unattainable goal. How could I possibly walk sixty miles? I was out of shape. I hadn't worked out in a long time. I felt overwhelmed. I was definitely starting at zero.

I decided to get un-stuck. I realized that major changes don't happen all at once—that I could make small changes every day which would add up to big changes. The first day, I looked at the Avon Web site and developed a training plan—the first chunk. The second day, I went to the shoe store and just walked around and looked—second chunk. The third day, I went back and bought a pair of walking shoes—third chunk. The fourth day I strolled around my neighborhood. I was pretty proud of myself and knew I was on my way—fourth chunk.

I remember the first day I walked a mile. I did a little celebration dance in my garage as I walked back into my home. I think that's the day I realized, "Oh my gosh, I can really do this!"

By May, I was walking Redstone Canyon—6.5 miles up (and I do mean *up*—I live in Colorado) and 6.5 miles back down, two or three days a week.

When it came time for the Walk, Colorado was having a heat wave. It was around one hundred degrees the entire weekend. I couldn't help but wonder if my training, chunk by chunk, had prepared me for sixty miles in the searing heat.

With each mile I walked with that intense sun beating me up, I got closer to my goal. At each rest stop, I'd see women on stretchers being rehydrated intravenously. I saw a few taken to the hospital. Sweep vans came by regularly to transport those who could not finish the day's miles to that night's tent city. I was determined to hang tough. I was determined to keep going. I was determined to finish. I'd grab a Gatorade and a bottle of water and keep going.

On the third day, I remember the feeling when I came to the "Welcome to Boulder" sign. I knew that a huge chunk was behind me, and that there were only a few more miles to go to get to the finish line. I knew there would be people lining the path, cheering us in. I focused on that last chunk.

I finished every one of those sixty miles, and raised $4000 to help fight breast cancer. I'd gone after this goal one chunk at a time. Even now, when I drive to Boulder, I find it astounding that I walked that distance. The key is to take a big thing and break it down into a series of small, doable action steps; then you focus on them one at a time.

Whether you are going after a huge goal, beginning a major project, or making a big change, chunk it down. Ask yourself, "What's today's part?" And put your focus there.

You can only make progress today. Don't get overwhelmed by the big picture—the, "How will I get there?" Just do today's chunk, plan tomorrow's chunk, and you *will* move toward accomplishing your goal.

Wright

But don't people usually start worrying when they get overwhelmed?

Diamond

You bet they do. And worrying is a dream-zapping behavior. It keeps us stuck. It focuses us on the worst possible outcome and gives that outcome our energy. It keeps us focused on what we *don't* want instead of what we *do* want.

I was watching *Everybody Loves Raymond* one night. Raymond had anguished over what to buy his dad for his birthday, and finally came up with what he thought was the perfect gift—a fish tank. He went out and bought his father a terrific fish tank, and filled it with fish. His father loved it! Raymond was so happy.

Later that night, he and his wife were in bed talking about his father's birthday party. Debra was commenting on how much Raymond's dad had loved the fish tank. Suddenly, Raymond had a panicked expression on his face. He turned to Debra and said, "Oh, no! Now I have to top this next year! How am I going to be able to find something as good as this? This has really raised Dad's expectations. Now I'm gonna have to find something even better next year!"

Debra sanely replied, "Well, Raymond, you don't have to worry about it for another year."

I was amazed by his response—it so clearly captures the essence of worrying. "Oh, no!" he said, "You clearly don't understand worrying— this means I have a whole year to worry about it!"

Does this sound familiar? Oh, I know *not you*, but don't we know people like this? Heck, I used to be one. My first reaction to change or to something unexpected was to catastrophize. I would zero in on all the things that could go wrong—all I had to lose—and I'd start to worry.

Then, about twenty years ago, a colleague, Dan Lumpkin, asked me a critical question. He asked, "How's that working for you?"

I found that question both profound and annoying. Of course it wasn't working for me! Staying stuck and being overwhelmed were not working. Not going after my dreams was not working. Worrying and catastrophizing were not working.

Yet, that question was a turning point for me. It came at a time in my life when I was in the midst of learning about the power of thought, the law of attraction, about taking personal responsibility— and I used it to help transform my life.

Letting go of worry takes commitment. It takes discipline. It takes courage. It takes a deep knowing that no matter what happens in your life, you are greater than any set of circumstances. Don't let the vortex of worry suck you down and keep you from your goals and dreams. Go for the best possible outcome.

Be like an oyster. The oyster is normally a placid creature, but occasionally small grains of sand work their way inside its shell and begin irritating it. At first, the oyster tries to get rid of them and when it finds it can't, it doesn't obsess, and it doesn't worry. It settles down and creates one of the most exquisite things in the world—a pearl.

No matter what situation you find yourself in, it's up to you to let go of worry and negativity and to get busy making pearls out of the situation. Instead of focusing on the worst-case scenario, I suggest that you focus on the *best-case scenario*, and then take the first step toward making that happen.

Wright

As we come to the end of our time together, what final message would you like to leave with our readers?

Diamond

The success you crave is within your reach! Know who you are. Be true to yourself. Decide what you want. Go after it with your heart and your soul. Be willing to grow. Use the power of thought. Leverage your talents and passion. Do what it takes. Chunk it down. Focus on today's part. Get out of your own way. Let go of worry. And take the time to celebrate your success!

About the Author

Ava Diamond is not your "run of the mill" speaker. She definitely "rocks the status quo." Her style? Gutsy and provocative. Her insights? Deep and thought-provoking. Her process? To shatter beliefs and obstacles that hold people and organizations back, and then unleash their creativity and energy to help them move beyond their previous limits to wild success. Her results? Transformational with bottom-line impact.

People walk away from her programs with powerful ideas and the inspiration it takes to implement them. They leave ready to take their lives and their businesses to new heights. Ava has worked with a "who's who" of American business, including IBM, Pepsico, Microsoft, Hewlett-Packard, and AT&T, as well as with associations and governments.

Ava Diamond
The Diamond Success Group
2420 Cedarwood Drive, Suite 200
Fort Collins, CO 80526
Phone: 970.224.3015
Fax: 970.224.2874
E-mail: ava@avadiamond.com
www.avadiamond.com
www.feistywomen.com